Pretty Good for a Woman

"*Pretty Good for a Woman*"

The Enigmas of Evelyn Scott

D. A. CALLARD

W·W·NORTON & COMPANY · New York · London

Library of Congress Cataloging in Publication Data

Callard, D. A.
Pretty good for a woman.
1. Scott, Evelyn, 1893–1963   —Biography.
2. Novelists, American—20th century—Biography.
I. Title.
PS3537.C89Z62   1985   813'.52 [B]   85–15226

ISBN 0-393-02276-5

W. W. Norton & Company, Inc., 500 Fifth Avenue, New York, N.Y. 10110
W. W. Norton & Company Ltd., 37 Great Russell Street, London WC1B 3NU

1 2 3 4 5 6 7 8 9 0

A line never expresses a life. Life is not linear. Wherefore the conventional biography is a fraud, and I have attempted to avoid the imposture [. . .] My friend Stieglitz used to say 'no one ever changes'. On the level of essence this is true: all I ever became was implicit in my earliest hour of 'revelation'. All my search for methodology to reach the truth was already present in the child making a continent of his body in the bath. Another beloved friend, Reinhold Niebuhr, when I asked him why he did not write his life, answered, 'no man writing his autobiography can help lying'. But the lie as one bespeaks one's life can reveal the truth. The lie can depict the man as faithfully as the sincerest statement.

Memoirs of Waldo Frank

Contents

Illustrations

Picture Credits

The author and publishers would like to thank the following for permission to reproduce illustrations: Richard Dalby for no. 17; André Deutsch Ltd for no. 18; Humanities Research Center, Austin, Texas for nos 1, 2, 3, 4, 5, 6 and 9; the International Institute for Social History, Amsterdam for nos 15 and 16; the Thomas Merton Studies Center for nos 13 and 14; New Directions Publishing Corporation for no. 12 (photo by Irving Wellcome); Paula Scott for no. 10; the Estate of Alfred Stieglitz for no. 11. All other photographs are from the author's own collection.

Introduction and
Acknowledgements

Evelyn Scott participated in almost every strand of
American intellectual life during the interwar years: the Greenwich Village revolt, the Stieglitz group, the European expatriate
scene, the art colonies of Taos and Santa Fé, feminism, anarchism, the rise of literary communism and the emergence of the
loose group known as the Southern Renaissance. She was
instrumental in the introduction of Joyce's work to America and
in the elevation of William Faulkner from the rank of minor
Southern writer to major novelist. She wrote a dozen adult books,
two books of verse and a play, yet she is mysteriously absent from
most memoirs of the period and from almost all critical surveys.

My interest in her stemmed from a chance discovery. I had
often been curious about a shop, which stood only half a mile
away from my house. Perched on the roadside in a waste tract of
rubble, nettles and fireweed, it emanated the peculiar silent
loneliness characteristic of an Edward Hopper painting. Inside,
unpriced objects were piled at random to be sifted by the
purchaser and a price decided by haggling with the owner, who
lived in voluntary squalor in rooms above the premises to which
customers would be invited to view the costlier treasures and to
drink strong sweet tea, in which the teabag would be left floating.

He was an enigmatic man; a former high-ranking Civil Servant
who had been an acquaintance of many prominent literary figures
of the thirties and forties. Now in old age, his ideal seemed to be
some kind of stasis in which interesting objects, conversation
partners and suitable reading material would materialise before

his inert frame. Running his kind of shop was probably the closest approximation to this. His stock was usually brought to him by one of his many contacts in the trade and invariably left the shop as it came in, unrestored and unchanged except by a veneer of dust.

Some years ago I called in to find he had acquired several thousand books from a storeroom clearance by a friend who had a bookshop somewhere in Camden. Since I supplemented my income by dealing in books I spent several fruitful afternoons sifting through the boxes dotted around the shop, and in a box beneath a billiard table I came across a novel called *Bread and a Sword*, an author's copy heavily amended 'for a future revised edition'. The book had been published by Scribner in America and it was written in a style somewhere between stream-of-consciousness and the experiments of German expressionism. The author was a woman of whom I had never heard called Evelyn Scott.

In Kunitz and Haycraft's *Twentieth-Century Authors* she was granted a lengthy, respectful entry, to which was appended a photograph of an attractive, wide-mouthed woman with luminous eyes. When I returned to the shop, I looked for more of her books and located several. Moreover, I discovered three manuscript drafts of the first part of a novel entitled *Before Cock Crow*.

The books exhibited a bewildering variety of contrasts and it was difficult to believe that they had been written by the same person. *Bread and a Sword* was a stylistically ingenious but flawed study of two poverty-stricken American artists in France, torn between the demands of economic survival on the one hand and political ideology on the other. An immense two-volume novel ironically entitled *A Calendar of Sin* used a Dos Passos technique in depicting a loosely related set of financial and sexual dramas in the period of reconstruction following the American Civil War. Another novel, *Breathe Upon These Slain*, explored the downfall of an English middle-class family in Sussex. The novel in manuscript was a disappointment and I read only a dozen pages before giving up the struggle. It was a story set in the French Revolution, and was ruined by an archaic rendition of French into English, full of thees, thous and Georgian slang. The published novels were interesting, but greatness eluded them. They returned to my shelves, undisturbed for another year.

A year later I was in a public library reading *The Times Literary Supplement* when, in the 'Information Please' column, I noticed an entry from an American woman researcher requesting information on the whereabouts of correspondence between Evelyn Scott and Lola Ridge. I answered the enquiry with a letter detailing my discovery of Scott manuscripts in a junkshop, a fact which seemed to suggest that the chance of the correspondence having survived was not high. As an afterthought, I enquired whether the researcher could tell me anything about Evelyn Scott.

I received a detailed reply, followed by a brief note informing me that the correspondence had been located at the Humanities Research Center at Austin, Texas, which had a large collection of Scott manuscripts. After some correspondence with that institution I sold them the material in my possession and assumed that was the end of the affair.

But curiosity dictated that it was not to be so. A *TLS* enquiry of my own elicited some interesting but apparently contradictory facts. On a visit to America I called at Evelyn Scott's birthplace, Clarksville, Tennessee, half expecting to find a small statue, or at least a plaque, only to find that she was forgotten there too. Eventually I visited the Humanities Research Center at Austin where, among the voluminous papers of the Scott archive, the thread of her strange, ultimately tragic career was pieced together.

My thanks must go to a number of people and organisations who have helped me in the course of my investigations: to Edward Allatt, Peggy Bach, Dr Robert Belflower, Kay Boyle, Paul F. Browning, Linda Bye, Dr John H. Clark, Richard Dalby, Claire de Silver, Richard Drinnon, the Federal Bureau of Investigation, Bill Gannett, Michael Gannett and Ruth Gannett Kahn, Geoffrey Grigson, Claire MacNamee, Paul Mariani, Michael Mott, Ronald Orr-Ewing, Victoria Orr-Ewing, Elaine Sproat, Christine Welch, Neda M. Westlake, Jonathan Williams, Francis Wyndham, the Yorkshire Arts Association.

Thanks also to the many librarians who co-operated (a full list may be found in the bibliography) and especially to Ellen Dunlap of the Humanities Research Center at Austin and Rudolf De Jong of the International Institute for Social History in Amsterdam, both of whose institutions I was privileged to visit.

I am grateful to Evelyn Scott's daughter-in-law and literary heir, Paula Scott, for her patience, co-operation and courage in revealing what were painful areas of her past and for granting permission to reproduce copyright material by Evelyn Scott. Similar thanks must be extended to Ian Ballantine, who granted permission to reproduce letters by Emma Goldman, and to Francis Wyndham for permission to reproduce letters by Jean Rhys. The letter from *What the Woman Lived: Selected Letters of Louise Bogan 1920–1970* (Harcourt Brace Jovanovich, 1973) is reprinted with permission of Ruth Limmer as trustee of the estate of Louise Bogan. Quotations from Thomas Merton's writings are courtesy of the Sheldon Press and the quotation from Kay Boyle is reprinted by permission of her agent, A. Watkins, Inc.

I

A Background in Tennessee

AT THE TURN of the century Clarksville, Tennessee, was a town of approximately ten thousand inhabitants, most of whom depended directly or indirectly on tobacco cultivation for their livelihood. Here, on January 17, 1893, Evelyn Scott was born and christened Elsie Dunn, the only child of Seely and Maude Thomas Dunn. In the marked social stratifications of Clarksville, the Dunns were among the few local families who could reasonably lay claim to membership of the 'Southern aristocracy'. Social behaviour in this class was rigidly codified and it is no accident that Dorothy Dix, for many years the arbiter of American etiquette, was a product of Clarksville. But beneath surface behaviour ran a deep strain of individualism, both in economic practice and in personal behaviour, and the usual range of libidinal and extramarital activity flourished and was countenanced, so long as it was not made public. Even when interracial, adultery and illegitimacy were acceptable if discreet; divorce and cohabitation were not.

Clarksville had not then produced any artist of more than local significance, yet within a dozen years this small town and its hinterland were to give birth to Evelyn Scott, Caroline Gordon and Robert Penn Warren. This efflorescence is not surprising, given the social importance of amateur artistic accomplishment among the upper classes. Though H. L. Mencken damned the south as 'the Sahara of the Bozart', the Clarksville bourgeois had a strong appreciation of artistic achievements of the past. But here, as in social mores, formality ruled.

Maude Thomas, Elsie Dunn's mother, was the child of a rich and unorthodox family. Her grandfather had been a Captain Joseph Thomas who had settled in the vicinity of Clarksville in 1829. He was a cultured man, a Jacksonian and idealist in youth who had made a moderate fortune in his heyday which he watched ebb in his declining years. Disillusioned with earlier aspirations, he ended his days running a school with his wife for instruction in the classics.

His son, Edwin Thomas, continued the radical tradition and was more financially successful than his father. He took an early stand against slavery and freed his own slaves. This, together with his non-combatant status in the Civil War, earned him the disapproval of more conventional citizens. But his business acumen was sufficient to purchase the Gracie Mansions, the huge, gloomy Greek-revival house in which Evelyn Scott was born. Her memoir of childhood, *Background in Tennessee*, suggests a naïveté in Edwin Thomas' aspirations, which were fuelled by his shrewd speculations in the tobacco trade:

It was the tobacco that had allowed it; the tobacco that had blessed him; the tobacco which had permitted him to purchase an estate. Tobacco made it possible for him to indulge ingenuous aspirations, and become an 'art collector'. It encouraged him to exceed his type in his ambition for his daughters, whom he proposed to convert into academic painters, literary creators, bluestockings. They were to carry on a tradition which he had, vaguely, inherited from his mother's mother.

The dreams of Edwin Thomas collapsed in later life like his father's, and he died at sixty with barely enough money to settle his debts. His wife, Fredonia McGinty, had been born in a log cabin near Clarksville of Ulster Protestant stock, a blood line which was converted by delusions of social grandeur to a lineage of Irish kings. In reality she was heir to a tradition of primitive pioneering, in strong contrast to the liberal, aristocratic Thomases. Their daughter, Maude Thomas, was no log cabin pioneer. She was too cultured and literate to be characterised as a 'Southern belle', but too lively and attractive to be labelled a 'bluestocking'. However, she was a product of her class and time, and never questioned the privileges of her station or the hypocritical social coaes which she adhered to. A sad, helpless victim of her upbringing, she was in no way prepared for reversion to the role of log cabin pioneer which was to be forced upon her.

Her husband, Seely Dunn, had Yankee parents though he had been born and raised in the South and this fact weighed against him in a society where the Yankee came usually as exploiter and carpet-bagger. He was a heavy-set man given to drinking bouts and occasional philandering, whose marriage to Maude Thomas had become a matter of form within a relatively short space of time. Like his father, he had made a career in railroad administration and had risen to become the youngest Division Superintendent in the USA. He also had a talent for disastrous business ventures. The Thomas family fortune was declining, and the marriage of Maude Thomas to Seely Dunn exhausted itself of affection so rapidly that one assumes it to have been morganatic rather than a love match. But the alliance failed to regenerate family finances and the young, acutely precocious Elsie Dunn grew up with the rankling knowledge that her parents' marriage was a sham and that the wealth underpinning their social position was rapidly eroding. In spite of this, *Background in Tennessee* portrays an Edenic world and it is likely that the full extent of the predicament was not apparent until the family was forced to move to New Orleans, close to Seely Dunn's parents.

Though Northerners, Oliver Milo Dunn and Harriet Marcy Seely Dunn had been resident in New Orleans for most of their lives. Oliver Dunn was General Superintendent of the Southern lines of the Illinois Central Railroad, a scrupulously honest businessman whose temperament was close to saintliness. Harriet Dunn's mental condition had deteriorated to near madness, a state manifesting itself in an obsession with hygiene and an extreme self-willedness. In 1922 the couple were found dead of gas asphyxiation in their New Orleans house. Though recorded as accidental death, it was generally understood to have been a simultaneous murder and suicide on the part of Oliver Dunn, who had been driven beyond the limits of endurance by his wife's deranged behaviour.

Such an unusual group of ancestors might be expected to produce an unusual child; Evelyn recognised this in her autobiographical entry in *Twentieth-Century Authors*:

If my mother, Southern from the seventeenth century, had not married a Yankee whose ancestors were from Boston and New York State, I might not have been impelled, as I was, to protest the lingering antebellum tradition under which I grew up [...] 'both literally and metaphorically', I have travelled far from the South of my childhood. But I owe it to the South, that I still prize most, in myself and in others, a man's control of his own spirit and mind – man's self-direction in the development of an inner life. And I owe it to the South that I never did, and do not now, see virtue in any proposal to make people 'good' by force. The frail Puritan in me has died, and I hope will never be reborn.

To influences of family and social background must be added the long shadow of the Civil War. It was then within living memory, and a macabre kudos was attached to having ancestors who had died in battle for the Cause. Evelyn's grandparents were non-combatants – worse, one grandfather had been a Yankee non-combatant. This background made possible the rigorously objective attitude of her later fiction of Southern history. She did not embrace the conception of romantic defeat, so firmly embedded in Southern psychology and colouring the overwhelmingly partisan bulk of Civil War literature.

The apparently timeless and secure idyll of *Background in Tennessee* was set in a world whose economic mainstays were collapsing. The early years of the twentieth century were difficult ones for the Dunn family and their peers, and eventually Seely Dunn made one bad investment too many. When Elsie Dunn was fourteen, the family was forced to abandon the Gracie Mansions and, after a brief sojourn in St Louis, settled in New Orleans. Here, her inchoate adolescent rebellion would harden over the next six years, until she committed an act which would exile her from her background for ever.

2

The Family as Nightmare - 1

A COMMON THREAD in much of Evelyn's work is the oppressive nature of the family. No solid biographical evidence remains beyond oblique hints and references, but there is little doubt that her bleak vision of family life derived from personal experience. Neither Mr nor Mrs Dunn seemed to have been the equal of their precocious only child. At fifteen Elsie Dunn wrote a letter, including her age, to the New Orleans *Times-Picayune*, advocating the legalisation of prostitution as a means of controlling venereal disease. Even in the context of liberal New Orleans mores, this must have raised eyebrows among the Dunns' social peers. She then wrote a propagandist novel on that theme and later commented, 'The indelicacy of the proposal upset my family, as the atrocious style of the manuscript would embarrass me at present could it be reproduced.' In the same interview, conducted in 1931, she said that she began writing fiction at the age of seven as a release for her 'overcharged emotionalism', and it is likely that this emotionalism found constant expression in her everyday behaviour.

Mr Dunn responded with genial, uncomprehending paternalism. In *Escapade*, where Mr Dunn is transparently veiled under the pseudonym of 'Uncle Alec', she wrote:

At that time Uncle Alec, in whom I always wanted to confide, kept me at a kindly distance. He could never bear to have me serious with him. If I tried to talk about myself he made a sympathetic jest of my ideas. Then he gazed at me, smiling, patted my head and was wistfully humorous about life. Life was too much of a muddle. Better not attempt the impossibility of a solution. He wanted me to be happy. I know now that his sense of responsibility in regard to me related only to my virginity. That is what I always felt. The love of those among whom one had been reared is usually not love at all. One can die inwardly without any of them being aware of it.

This cry of misunderstood adolescence was amplified in the case of Elsie Dunn by her status as an only child. She wrote that in New Orleans, 'that conviction of loneliness and misunderstanding so frequent with only children became confirmed in me'. The miserable years in New Orleans were exacerbated by chronic adolescent shyness and a bluestocking image gained by virtue of prodigious reading, which 'inspired me with simultaneous ambitions to become a writer, a painter, an actress and a disciple of Pavlova, Tolstoy, Nietzsche, Bergson and Karl Marx all at once'.

Her mother dominated her upbringing. When Evelyn told an interviewer that her home was 'saturated in bookishness', she referred to her mother's cultivated sensibility. Mrs Dunn transferred much thwarted marital affection to her daughter, though was as uncomprehending of her as was her husband. Many of her physical characteristics, her diminutive stature and large grey eyes, were inherited by Elsie Dunn, who also shared her mother's nervousness, shyness and finely tuned temperament. Reduced family circumstances offended Mrs Dunn's sense of social propriety, as did the public mental imbalance of her mother-in-law. Mrs Dunn's paranoiac cast of mind assumed that she was a constant subject of everyday gossip. Without inner resources to deal with these problems herself, much of their weight fell on to her classically anguished child.

Though finances were straitened, the Dunns were some way from the street. Mr Dunn was still well enough endowed to send Elsie to the Sophie Newcombe Preparatory School, an establishment dedicated to the schooling of Southern belles and 'the finest girls' school in Louisiana'. She studied art briefly at the Sophie Newcombe Art School and for a short period became the youngest girl student to enrol at Tulane University. Her educational career was not conspicuously successful by her own admission, because she was temperamentally incapable of submitting to formal discipline. Evelyn later regretted her failure to study art and in her novels the artist was posited as the supreme example of the individual at war with society. In effect, she was almost entirely self-taught and her rejection of formal education in favour of personal intellectual exploration coloured her literary output. On a basic level she was a poor speller who took a cavalier attitude to rules of grammar and punctuation. And like that other autodidact, D. H. Lawrence, the subject matter of her books was constantly innovatory and she was to explore almost every literary genre.

Like many outsiders her rebellion first took the form of romanticising the outcast. As a child in Clarksville she had been fascinated by its apparently picturesque poor white community and the equally exotic enclave of 'Niggertown'. In New Orleans her revolt found political expression in the growing demand for female emancipation. Given the view of womanhood current in Louisiana this was radical enough, but it failed to satisfy the young Elsie Dunn:

> I have traced, at least to my own satisfaction, the course of small events which first aroused me to awareness of my status as a member of a class oppressed by the law. Before I was sixteen, I had become an ardent feminist; at seventeen I became secretary of the then newly organised Woman's Suffrage Party of Louisiana. I was disillusioned in this enthusiasm chiefly because, in myself, the logic of protest was pursued to a catholic culmination, whereas in the women with whom I was associated (most of them mature), the demand for justice was very specifically made. I was ready to champion the negro, the social outcast, and to insist, after an imperfectly digested reading of Karl Marx, on the instant termination of industrial slavery – and the ladies who were disconcerted by my ardour did not agree.

Elsie Dunn was intellectually confined even in the relatively cultured environment of New Orleans. As she entered her twenties, unable to stomach formal education and with her nightmarish home life bringing her close to suicide, she was introduced to the man who would be the dominant influence on her life. Together they were to commit an act of existential suicide which would sever both from their past histories and current predicaments.

3

a.k.a.

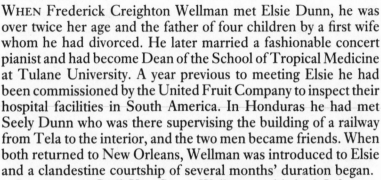

WHEN Frederick Creighton Wellman met Elsie Dunn, he was over twice her age and the father of four children by a first wife whom he had divorced. He later married a fashionable concert pianist and had become Dean of the School of Tropical Medicine at Tulane University. A year previous to meeting Elsie he had been commissioned by the United Fruit Company to inspect their hospital facilities in South America. In Honduras he had met Seely Dunn who was there supervising the building of a railway from Tela to the interior, and the two men became friends. When both returned to New Orleans, Wellman was introduced to Elsie and a clandestine courtship of several months' duration began.

In 1943, as Cyril Kay-Scott, Wellman published *Life is too Short*, an autobiography which contains substantial, though often distorted, information on his years with Evelyn Scott. Even allowing for exaggeration and self-aggrandisement, the book charts a remarkable career of a man who gained mention in *Who's Who in America* under both names he used.

He was born in 1874 in Independence, Missouri, and had a rigorous Puritan upbringing from which it would take many years to break free. After obtaining a medical degree he had married a woman of a similar background and had gone to Africa as a medical missionary. Here three of his children were born and he gained a reputation as an authority on tropical disease. His marriage had broken up when he turned against the Puritanism which his wife embraced more rigidly, and he became a roué, wandering Europe and moving in sophisticated circles, devoting

much energy to exerting his charm upon women. His friendship
with the concert pianist Edna Willis had begun on a boat bound
for New Orleans where he was to take up the post at Tulane. The
marriage was a precipitate affair and soon soured. Edna Willis
was an attractive woman, but Wellman soon found that she lacked
the sensitivity he thought he had perceived. She was a socialite
and had an excessive interest in vapid forms of social intercourse
which he despised. The Puritan died hard. As dean of a faculty,
Wellman could provide the status she required and the money to
maintain it.

Wellman was a powerful personality, an erudite man with a
multidisciplinary range of knowledge. He allowed his son to
describe him in the introduction to his book as an explorer,
linguist, anthropologist, bacteriologist, journalist, economist and
latter-day Renaissance man. He was also an egoist. Most of *Life is
too Short* is true, as far as verification is possible, and the distortions
in the book arise from omission rather than deliberate falsehood.
Paul Wellman, a son who by 1943 had become a successful
popular novelist and Hollywood screenwriter, admits this in his
introduction. 'By deliberate purpose he chose to live unconven-
tionally, and out of this has come great unhappiness which,
however, he never admits or discusses.' And a close reading of
Life is too Short gives a clear impression that while success is
magnified, failure is quietly ignored.

Wellman was the main lifelong influence on Evelyn's intellectual and personal development and *Background in Tennessee*
acknowledges his influence on her a decade after their 'divorce':

> While I was at school in New Orleans, the works of Stephen
> Crane, Frank Norris and Theodore Dreiser influenced me far
> more significantly than did my half-creole milieu, discussed
> idyllically in the stories of George Cable. And as I matured I
> owed more to conversations with Cyril Kay-Scott than to the
> accident of a residence in France or South America or North
> Africa.

The philosophy of Wellman/Scott/Kay-Scott (who at the end
of his life reverted to Wellman) was a self-created individualism.
He did not care for systematised beliefs and one of the aphorisms
in *Life is too Short* observes that, 'An ideology is just an idea that

has got out of hand'. He despised the Puritanism of his upbringing but rejected Freud and psychoanalysis as a panacea. He
underwent a religious experience in the isolation of Brazil which
taught him to pray once more but did not lead to the adoption of a
formulated faith. Though an advocate of personal freedom,
Bohemian antics were to appal him and the people most warmly
remembered in his book are unsophisticated natives of Africa or
Brazil.

In spite of a matrimonial career which was to include six
'wives', he was not a philanderer or a promiscuous man. Evelyn
denied vehemently in *Escapade* that he had taken advantage of
her: 'It is the usual indignity. If I had been older I would have
been called a "vampire". As it is, I was "seduced". In any case I
am not to be allowed any decent self-responsibility for my acts.'

The courtship lasted for about four months and eventually
could not be concealed from Mr and Mrs Dunn. Elsie finally told
her mother that she planned to elope with Wellman and urged her
to end her own unhappy marriage. Mrs Dunn reacted characteristically with hysterics and a tragi-comic scene in which she
threatened to shoot herself with one of her husband's rifles. Yet,
in spite of prior warning, the couple failed to act to prevent their
daughter's flight.

So as not to arouse suspicion, Wellman told his wife that he was
going on a fishing trip. The subterfuge worked, but meant that he
was unable to take more than the minimum of clothing and
possessions. On December 26, 1913, a few weeks before Elsie's
twenty-first birthday, they eloped at dawn, fleeing north to New
York then taking a boat to London, where they settled as man and
wife in Bloomsbury. It was the plan of both to go to the tropics
but, Wellman reasoned, Mr Dunn as a railroad man would have
little difficulty in tracing them unless they took a circuitous route.
Cyril Kay-Scott's account of events leading to the elopement is
surprisingly laconic, considering that he was abandoning a marriage, social status, personal comfort, a degree of wealth and a
distinguished career:

In Elsie Dunn I found one of the few women I had known up to
that time with whom I could discuss philosophy. She had an
unusually brilliant mind with which, had she been able to
develop the character and emotional stability to match, she

could have made herself a very famous woman. She did, in the years to come, attain fame through her books and, had she treasured fewer personal caprices, possibly might have become our greatest American writer. I didn't know all this then; but I liked to talk to her. She was young, physically attractive, unlearned, and original, and that appealed to me. I thought she might prove interesting. She was probably more interested in getting away from her family than she was in me. A man and a woman toasting marshmallows in a deserted drawing room, walking in moonlight, or discussing American realistic fiction beginning with Frank Norris, are outworn subjects, and I pass over them; for, at the end of a few months, the only really important thing that turned the scale was, as in the case of my first wife, that Miss Dunn was the only woman I knew at the time who would consent to go to the tropics with me. I was glad it was to be someone who didn't bore me.

Perhaps closer to the truth is an account given in a letter Cyril wrote to Lola Ridge in 1919: 'We were both contemplating making away with ourselves when we met. I held her in my arms for a year before she wanted to live.' The account written in 1943 reflects more on events subsequent to the flight than on the true state of mind of both parties at the time of elopement.

When the disappearance became public, a mammoth scandal erupted in the yellow press of the South which percolated as far as the English gutter press. Walking along a London street, Wellman read a lurid account of himself and his exploits and felt that a little more subterfuge might be necessary. The main story of the time was the discovery of the bodies of the failed Scott expedition to Antarctica, and so he took the name of Scott. The Cyril Kay was taken from a contemporary matinée idol, but how Elsie achieved the transformation to Evelyn is unrecorded.

In New Orleans general wisdom laid the blame for the outrage on Wellman and he was portrayed as a vile seducer and probable white slaver. The latter was a current bogey in the public imagination and the Mann Act had been passed some years earlier, forbidding the transportation of minors across state lines for 'immoral purposes'. Wellman's highly developed instinct for self-preservation had failed him in eloping with Elsie five weeks before her twenty-first birthday, and the enraged, deserted Edna

Willis publicly threatened him with prosecution under the Act should he be caught. Mr Dunn discovered that he too had a thespian streak and offered rewards which he could not afford to pay, threatening horsewhipping should the couple set foot in New Orleans again. Mrs Dunn entered a bout of hysterics which would last many, many weeks.

There had been no seduction and, until both were on the boat for England, Elsie had been 'a virgin with contempt for a view of chastity as psychological rather than of the spirit'. With new names they had completely estranged themselves from their pasts, but the danger still remained that their pasts might catch up with them. So, Cyril made arrangements with the British Museum to collect entomological specimens in Latin America and passportless, stateless and nearly penniless, the couple set sail on the *Blücher* for a new life in Brazil.

4

Brazilian Escapade

WHEN THE *Blücher* docked at Rio de Janeiro, Evelyn was already pregnant. They had little luggage and she had dresses suitable only for an American winter. Between them they had seven hundred dollars and three books, a volume of Shelley, a volume of Keats and *War and Peace*.

They checked in at a cheap hotel called the Rio Branco whose rough bar, which adjoined the dining room, terrified Evelyn. Cyril was fluent in Portuguese but Evelyn was not and her isolation and the enormity of what she had done became impressed on her. Ideas of collecting entomological specimens proved unrealistic as their money dwindled and Cyril, former medical missionary and college dean, was forced into such desperate and unfamiliar stratagems as carrying luggage at the railway station and labouring on road gangs at forty cents a day. He had no credentials relating to former careers and was loth to reveal his past identity. Eventually he found work as a bookkeeper in a Singer Sewing Machine store, a job which paid twenty dollars a week and allowed the couple to move to a better hotel. But their situation was not secure and Evelyn for some time considered working as a servant for a Brazilian family.

Cyril's job proved tiring, especially since he had to learn rudimentary bookkeeping from scratch. He was away for most of the day and Evelyn was a virtual prisoner in the hotel room for, if she went out, she found herself the object of unwanted advances by men speaking a strange language. Even in this 'better' hotel, conditions were less than opulent:

We have the same coarse fish fried in oil, the same indescribable meats, and when we request a little lettuce it comes to us
half-covered with sand, with oil served in a broken cruet.
There is frequently a fly in the stew, and sometimes even a
roach [...] In the indescribable toilets there are signs which
request the guests not to throw paper in the bowls, cock-
roaches rattle through the empty tin provided as a waste-paper
receptacle, and from a nail depends a soiled cloth with which to
wipe off the wooden seat. There is one tub in the hotel, but I am
too frightened of disease to bathe in it.

This account appeared in *Escapade*, the memoir of Brazil which
Evelyn published in 1923. The strange background to the exile is
barely touched upon and all the reader learns is that a well-born
and educated American woman is reduced to poverty and illness
in a strange country. It is highly subjective and studded with
asterisks marking suppressed passages, many of which relate to
Evelyn's sexuality and pregnancy, but an almost equal amount are
detailed reports on that fertile region of American repression: the
comfort station, rest room, bathroom or john. This was a recurrent area of interest and future letters from Europe and elsewhere
betray a fascinated repulsion with accommodations made by
other cultures with the fact of defecation. The book, strictly a
memoir and according to Evelyn 'absolutely truthful', contains
several fictional devices, and some reviewers treated it as fiction
when it appeared. Though the narrator remains anonymous, she
disguised her parents as 'Uncle Alec' and 'Aunt Nannette'. Cyril
was further renamed 'John' and her Brazilian-born son Creighton was called 'Jackie'.

After some months as bookkeeper, Cyril was promoted to
auditor and the couple moved to a private boarding house. Here
Evelyn wrote home, telling of her whereabouts and pregnancy,
and began to study Portuguese seriously. Cyril was rapidly
promoted again, this time to superintendent, and there was
another move, northward to Natal, an area with a more healthy
climate.

Both Mr and Mrs Dunn replied to the letter home. Mrs Dunn
wrote a letter full of reproaches. She was still hysterical and
smarting from the social disgrace her daughter had caused. The
volume of publicity, much of it encouraged by Edna Willis, had

made life in New Orleans intolerable. She received little sympathy from Evelyn in *Escapade*: 'The simple fact of course is that I love John more than I have ever loved Nannette, and that I am willing to make sacrifices in order to be with him. As yet I don't consider that I have made any. It somehow pleases my vanity to know that I no longer have a respectable reputation.'

The two letters from Seely Dunn exhibit surprising sanguinity from a man who had been stalking New Orleans with a horsewhip. He forgave both with the confession to Cyril that, 'under different circumstances, I might have done the same thing myself'. The motives behind these conciliatory gestures were to be apparent only when Maude Dunn acted on her daughter's invitation to visit Brazil.

The pregnancy was difficult, and the combination of illness and cultural isolation caused Evelyn to suffer sensations of identity loss and 'invisibility'. At times, pain seemed the only fact which convinced her of her continued existence. In Natal Creighton was born on October 26, 1914; delivered without anaesthetic by a Dr Januario who Cyril claimed was 'the best doctor in town'. Evelyn found his person and bedside manner, replete with sexual innuendo, repulsive. Whether due to his ineptitude, to physiological factors or simply to the absence of adequate surgical equipment, complications following birth left Evelyn an invalid for the duration of her stay in Brazil and affected her health lifelong. A later operation had to be carried out by an American medical missionary to sew up lacerated ligaments resulting from the birth. When the couple returned to New York in 1919 a further operation was needed and she was treated for the same complaint in 1930. In 1951 Evelyn attributed her health problems to 'childbirth and hard work', and it is probable that the injuries she sustained prevented her from having more children.

For much of the pregnancy Cyril's work required him to be away from home and Evelyn was cared for by two native servant girls. One of these, Petronilla, gave birth to an illegitimate child without complications. Contrasting the two births in his autobiography Cyril commented that 'civilised women are biologically incompetent', but he failed to mention that the child died of neglect soon after birth. Evelyn was at the mercy of Petronilla, whom she hated, and her only respite was a brief, unpleasant period in the clinic of a sanctimonious missionary doctor who performed the post-natal operation. And, no sooner were the birth and attendant complications over, than Mrs Dunn landed at Recife.

Little affection exited between Cyril and Maude Dunn even prior to the elopement and he caricatured her mercilessly in his first novel, *Blind Mice*. In *Life is too Short* he described her as 'the type of mother-in-law who believes a man is controlled solely by sexual attraction and, having lost hers, would attempt to capitalise the attractiveness of her daughter (whom she would always regard as a minor) in order to control a man through manipulation of that.'

Evelyn found her mother much changed. She was nervous, haggard and insisted on acting in a conspiratorial manner. Apart from worry and disgrace, Mr Dunn's business ineptitude had meant that all servants had been dispensed with and Mrs Dunn had been reduced to doing the laundry herself. In the context of Brazilian poverty she was grotesquely out of place, fighting a rearguard action to preserve the vestiges of her beauty by cosmetics and insistent on changing for a dinner which was frequently beans or manioc eaten from a tin billy. Yet Cyril could feel some sympathy for her situation, which is one of the most bizarre social declines ever recorded. Through no fault of her own she had slipped from Southern aristocratic ease to an existence barely above that of a Brazilian peon and this would be her status for some years to come.

Because of financial difficulties Mrs Dunn had come to Brazil on a one-way ticket; Seely Dunn had promised to send money for a return passage when available. But after her arrival he sent nothing, nor did he reply to her letters home. Mrs Dunn's nervous condition worsened and after a year her face was so devoid of pigmentation that vanity forced her to wear a veil. The servants contemptuously referred to her as 'the old one' and barely maintained politeness toward her. Then, fifteen months after arrival, she had word that Seely Dunn had divorced her for desertion, an act which casts light on his conciliatory view of the elopement. Shortly after the divorce he married a woman slightly older than his daughter, and the money for a return passage never arrived.

This news prompted torrential hysteria and suicide threats

from Maude Dunn. She was now stranded with Cyril and Evelyn and dependent on Cyril, the author of her misfortunes, for her daily bread.

Both women were adept hysterics and Cyril became used to returning to emotional chaos. He commented sourly, 'In isolation, women who can't make a bed, a pie or a garden seem to make situations. And, in my house, mother and daughter during my absence appeared to have daily occupied themselves in making them.' He came to feel that the present domestic arrangement was unhealthy for his son and also that to be a sales representative and rent collector for sewing machines was not the tropical adventure he had envisaged. So he hired two new servant girls and decided to begin a career as a rancher. This simply involved staking a claim to land, setting up house and beginning to farm. In the course of his travels he had met several who had become rich and determined that he should do the same.

In the interior he had discovered a thousand acres of unregistered land which he felt was promising. He duly entered homestead rights with the authorities, resigned from the Singer Company and began to prepare to move his household to Cercadinho and what was the central experience of the Brazilian exile.

5

Cercadinho

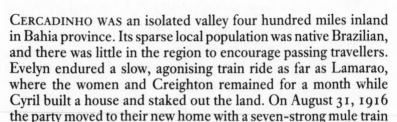

CERCADINHO WAS an isolated valley four hundred miles inland in Bahia province. Its sparse local population was native Brazilian, and there was little in the region to encourage passing travellers. Evelyn endured a slow, agonising train ride as far as Lamarao, where the women and Creighton remained for a month while Cyril built a house and staked out the land. On August 31, 1916 the party moved to their new home with a seven-strong mule train and ten men assisting.

The landscape was desolate but staggeringly beautiful and was to provoke the most memorably descriptive passages of *Escapade*. Even Mrs Dunn was entranced by the scenery, though she said that she would have preferred to see a few houses in it. When she saw the palm hut in which they were to live, she was rather disconcerted by the absence of glass windows.

Fortune smiled on the enterprise in its first year. Cyril planted a cash crop of manioc which made enough money to allow further investment. A new five-roomed mud and thatch house was built and from the surrounding countryside several squatters appeared who started smallholdings on the land and assisted with the massive task of cultivation. Cyril became enough of a *ranchero* to refer to them as 'my peons', though it is unlikely that he ever had sufficient surplus to pay them. Creighton's nurse, Stephania, lived with the family for several years in return for only bed and board, so fond was she of her charge. For most of this time Evelyn remained an invalid and Mrs Dunn passed from hysteria to a torpid acceptance of her peculiar fate.

There were good grounds for optimism and when the second manioc crop was a success, Cyril made the unfortunate decision to invest their accumulated capital in a hundred and thirty sheep. Within a short time, for no identifiable reason, the sheep began to die. The sky above the valley filled with vultures and, sensing failure, the squatters drifted away. Cyril continued to work the fields alone until his health, strained by several years of manual labour, broke and for a time he was in danger of dying. Characteristically this is unmentioned in his autobiography, so afraid was he of anything smacking of failure, but it was recorded in *Escapade*. For some time it seemed likely that none of them would leave Cercadinho alive, but Cyril's health rallied and he continued to farm as best he could. It was during this blackest period that he underwent the mystical experience which made Cercadinho so important to him in retrospect. *Life is too Short* asserts that 'Though not from the viewpoint of superficially showy danger and violence, yet in its sustained inner drama of initial success, then sudden failure, struggle, despair, hope, with final triumph and escape to freedom, Cercadinho was the greatest not only of my Brazilian adventures but perhaps of my life.'

Both he and Evelyn began to write. Much of *Escapade* gives the sense of having been transcribed from journal notes and Evelyn wrote several plays and dramatic sketches. From America Mrs Dunn, who saw Evelyn as vicarious actor of her own thwarted literary ambitions, had sent her a poetry magazine, probably Harriet Monroe's *Poetry*. Evelyn was certainly aware of the development of Imagism and contributed to both *Poetry* and *The Egoist* while still living in Brazil. The sequence published in *Poetry* in 1919, *Tropical Life*, is standard imagist verse and would be unremarkable but for the fact that its author was a young woman who was far removed from any literary milieu. As in *Escapade*, sensations of pain and fear predominate:

Mail on the Ranch

The old black man on the mule
Opens the worn saddle-bags
And takes out the papers.

From the outer world
The thoughts come stabbing,

To taunt, baffle, and stir me to revolt.
I beat against the sky,
Against the winds of the mountain;
But my cries, grown thin in all this space,
Are diluted with emptiness ...
Like the air,
Thin and wide,
Touching everything,
Touching nothing.

The subjective passages of *Escapade* reiterate the same loss of identity, a sensation which became almost constant following the failure of the ranch. This was the obverse, negative side of the pantheistic illuminations which Cyril experienced at the same time; his tending to hope while hers reached down to despair. The deep nihilism which many saw in both her art and personality was only confirmed by her suffering:

There is a time when pain is everything, when it has taken me so completely that I have not any longer the knowing of consciousness, and I think more than anything of being left alone, of peace, of a kind of extinct quietness. I do not wish to know any longer. I know too much already, and I am burdened with understanding a world which is mine only. I cannot draw into this horror those whom I love who have already too little happiness. But I wonder how it is possible to go on for ever carrying with me an unshared experience, the most profound that I have ever met.

The worst of it is that my body, which has betrayed me, also obliges me to exert myself on its behalf, and as there are no toilet facilities other than a large tin bucket, I have to drag myself to it. Then I understand that I am really not alive at all, that I am already dead, and what remains in the place of my will is a kind of ghost of sensation, disintegrated and moveless. My thoughts are torn from me by little fingers that dig deep, deep into my mind, into the regions of me most obscure to myself.

In the face of disaster, Mrs Dunn lapsed into a state of complete passivity; a somnambulism in which the simple act of boiling a kettle was too much for her. Her hands trembled constantly, she lived near to tears and handled the few surviving luxury items from her previous life as if they were talismans. The nature of conversations during the long evenings on the ranch gives scope for wild conjecture: the intelligent, neurotic, beautiful daughter and her child; her mother clinging to past familiarity like the Somerset Maugham character afraid of engulfment in the savagery of the jungle, and her daughter's lover, an erudite and cultivated man whose fallible strength was all that stood between his household and its extinction. Cyril's autobiography managed to evince some sympathy for Mrs Dunn, but this probably grew with hindsight:

So I suppose I was unjust, in my thoughts at least, to the poor lady. Her complete uselessness probably wasn't her fault. She had been carefully reared for that which no longer existed in her life; and there was a sort of pathetic irony in her situation. I say pathetic, and not tragic. Futility is pathetic: the realisation of futility is tragic. And I pitied her, which was a sort of unsolicited condescension in itself. Pity holds something of the same relation to sympathy that contempt does to disapproval. I tried always to be courteous, but mentally I am afraid I too often put down her acts meant as kindliness to skilful attempts to attract attention, and her demonstrations of affection to fear of being ignored.

To Evelyn she was a portent of the state to which her own enslavement to an imperfect physical body might lead; fear of becoming like her mother coloured their complex future relationship. The event which wakened Mrs Dunn from torpor was when the whole family caught lice. After this mortification she slipped over the borderline between hysteria and insanity and Cyril, after telling her that he would murder her if he had the nerve, refused to speak to her. By this time all were dressed in rags in which they slept. Baby Creighton had to be deloused or 'chiggered' on several occasions and this led to his being called 'Jigger' or 'Jigeroo', usually shortened to Jig: a nickname which stayed with him throughout his life.

A brief, comical respite came when Cyril found a diamond on his land. Diamond fever overcame the group with even Mrs Dunn joining the fruitless search for more. When later sold the stone proved to be low-grade and yielded only a hundred dollars, but the incident was used by Evelyn as the basis for her mystery thriller *Blue Rum*.

Deliverance from their predicament came when news filtered through that an American company had begun prospecting for manganese in the area. Cyril visited a neighbour, whose proudest possession was a very loud suit, and begged to borrow it. It proved to be a poor fit but, undaunted, Cyril had his hair cut, shaved and walked sixty-five kilometres to the prospector's camp, sleeping rough at nights. He pretended to have some mining experience and the subterfuge got him the job in spite of the fact that the superintendent thought his suit 'a scream'. After a few weeks' work there he obtained an advance and returned to Cercadinho, a saviour. For all their enmity, it seemed Mrs Dunn had always known that he could deliver them from the prospect of permanent exile. The ranch was abandoned, with some regret on Cyril and Evelyn's part, and the group made their way down to the railway station. Evelyn travelled sedated by morphine and the day after their arrival at Lamarao, they took a train to Villa Nova where Cyril was to be based. He was to be paid twenty-five American dollars weekly; more than enough to keep his family in comfort, and from this point much of the drama evaporates from the Brazilian story. The realistic part of *Escapade* ends with the train journey to Villa Nova, though the family remained in Brazil for two more years.

6

The Funniest Thing
I Ever Wrote

THE SEVENTH part of *Escapade* was a mysterious episode, apparently unrelated to the rest of the book, which began life as a playlet Evelyn had written on the ranch. She found *Escapade* an extraordinary difficult book to write and asserted that she had tried several times to fictionalise her Brazilian exile and had failed. 'I had to write it, and write it just as it was.'

Upton Sinclair, who in 1923 was a syndicated reviewer for the Hearst newspapers, wrote to Evelyn via her publisher with several queries. He had written an admiring review of *Escapade* but was curious how truthful an account the book gave. He recalled that he had once hoaxed the public himself with *The Journal of Arthur Stirling*, a pseudonymous potboiler supposedly the autobiography of a self-obsessed writer who commits suicide. The book had been enormously popular and triggered an epidemic of neo-Nietzscheanism among the many lost souls who identified with its hero.

The core of Sinclair's review had been an attack on the injustice of the Mann Act, a propagandist interpretation which irritated Evelyn. None the less she wrote back from Algeria where she was then living, thanking Sinclair for his interest and clarifying his questions. She avoided any interpretation of the book's ending, but confirmed that the realistic parts of the book were true.

Most of the book's admirers found the inclusion of 'Shadow Play' as a climax incomprehensible. Kay Boyle read the book and also queried its author. More than fifty years later she recalled, 'I know that I was critical of Evelyn's ending of *Escapade*. I do not remember the ending now, but I do remember her annoyance at my questioning of that ending. She asked me – by letter – if I had expected a golden ladder to descend from the clouds, with angels strumming their harps on it. I do not recall her explanation, but I know she considered the ending the right one.'

Evelyn was more forthcoming to her friend and confidante, Lola Ridge. Lola had been sent a draft of 'Shadow Play' in 1919, when Evelyn described it as, 'not the largest or most difficult thing I have ever attempted, but will be for me the most unduplicable as it represents all I think about everything'. She wrote to Lola in 1922 that she was struggling to write about Brazil and described her plan:

> It is an autobiography of myself in Brazil. Not like other autobiographies except in being written in the first person. It is broken into impressionistic bits, a page or so at a time and being purely objective in matters of environment – or rather nearly objective, becomes more and more subjective to almost free verse self-explanation, and is to end with dreams, the final one being a slightly revised Shadow Play. Shadow Play can be used at last and just in the way it ought for it absolutely represents my absolute at that period, having been written then. I never went through so many fits writing anything, and, but for Cyril, would have given it up, but he likes it best of anything.

Later that year Evelyn told Lola that the book was complete: 'The Brazilian book is DONE. It is the funniest thing I ever wrote. Not a novel at all, but a simple, mildly subjectified statement of the facts of the first three years of our life in Brazil, and if I did not have Cyril so strong for it, I would not know whether it was a book or not. It was an uncontrolled and unconscious performance as the mere necessity to state facts and to speak in the first person threw me off all the confidence five years have taught me.'

Cyril's enthusiasm for both Evelyn and *Escapade* had waned by 1943 when he dismissed it as 'being so subjective that it might well have been written in Newark, New Jersey'. His recollections of Evelyn in Brazil were principally her outbursts of nihilistic despair, in which she would beat her head with her fists and scream: 'If we all went crazy, we wouldn't have to realise our situation.' With hindsight he erected Creighton's nurse, Stephania, as heroine of the saga, whereas in *Escapade* she leaves the group with a concocted excuse shortly after arrival at the ranch. The two accounts are opposed in fact and method and no witness can verify which is closer to the truth. However, Cyril was present when Evelyn wrote *Escapade*, a mere eight years after the events described, whereas she had no opportunity to vet his memoir.

When she read *Life is too Short*, Evelyn was appalled by Cyril's account. She wrote to David Lawson:

And as my account of 'Cercadinho' is emotionally and factually accurate in every detail, I was floored to find the vile hardships he, myself and Jig endured there dismissed with a sort of flourish and a comment on the 'joys of feudalism', but they are not to be found in a mud and wattle hut that collapses, as that did in the rainy season! It is not pleasant to be obliged to build brushwood fires on the floor of a windowless and hearthless room in order to drive out gnats that sting so painfully you cannot endure them and prefer suffocation by woodsmoke to their bloody bite. In *Life is too Short* the house of adobes Cyril replaced the hut walls with, room by room, to the full extent of two rooms and a half – the kitchen had three walls and was open in front – is alluded to as though we left behind us there a commodious modern farm cottage, when there was not even a window glass to be had.

In 1955 she gave a late interpretation of the ending of *Escapade* consistent with earlier ones. The critic Lewis Gannett questioned the relevance of the chapter and Evelyn ascribed his aversion to what she called 'the beard chapter' as being Freudianly related to his background. She claimed that the ending expressed her nascent views on life and the impact of raw nature:

I think some who read *Escapade* tend to overlook its autobiographical character of fact on the one hand, and, on the other, supposing all said in the more naturalistic vein of the other chapters, draw back from fantasy as 'incongruous'.

It is *not* however if the book is first viewed as an account of my own life of that time. Shadow Play is commentary, and has in it *intimations* of all the philosophical developments of myself thenceforth. A character christianly formed looks on nature and, doing so realistically, finds it tragic: an occasion for the pity that is a moral luxury not often indulged in even by christian orthodoxy today – or then!

This tallies with the statement made thirty-five years earlier that it 'represented all I think about everything', a comment it is unlikely she would have remembered making. Yet, the significance of 'Shadow Play' was visible only to its author. The piece has no objective correlative and like a dream can support a variety of interpretations, or none.

In the opening scene a Monsieur Renard and a Mr Bulle are seated at a luxurious dining table with a Madame Dina. The first man is an elegant cosmopolitan, the second a coarse, vulgar figure. Both have bestial features; furry, pointed ears, a bushy tail, horns. Madame Dina is beautiful, sensual and sumptuously dressed. She flirts with Monsieur Renard.

A young man called Aaron who is also a rival for her affections enters and challenges Renard. Renard attempts to buy him off with stock exchange tips, but their progress toward a duel is interrupted by the appearance of a mob storming the house. The servants rush in, terrified, but Renard is unperturbed: 'Craven hearted servant, do you suppose that *I* know fear! Anyone can see that you belong to the lower classes ... It is the inrush of democracy, but the tide will recede.'

A mob armed with bills and overdue accounts breaks into the room. Mr Bulle bellows and makes for the crowd but is halted when one of them pulls out a red handkerchief and waves it before him. Aaron asks how much is owed, is told and pulls out his pockets. They are empty. The crowd demands blood but Renard is unperturbed and pays them off contemptuously with gold pieces which he scatters on the floor.

Aaron is contritely grateful and suggests that he and Madame Dina will work for Renard until the debt is paid. But Madame Dina acts the Southern belle: '*I* work? *I* link my name with that of a failure? Never! I have my pride also – and beside I have no desire to interfere with the process of natural selection. Monsieur Renard, my natural protector, your arm.'

The couple and Mr Bulle leave. The servants demand wages from Aaron and begin to steal the silver cutlery. A policeman enters and demands that order be restored. Aaron indicates that they are welcome to the cutlery, but it is pointed out that it has never been paid for. The policeman says that if the plates are not paid for, then they are not Aaron's but his by law. Since possession is nine points of the law and he is the law, the rest must follow.

Aaron steps forward and announces the establishment of a higher law. 'In place of hard and fast rules we have established the judgement of inspiration.' He is mysteriously transformed into a prophet and the house into a darkened cathedral. A woman is distantly illuminated, classically robed. She reveals herself to be Madame Dina. The servants hail her as divine. They dress in Madame Dina's garments and, on Aaron's instruction, place their pilfered silver cutlery on the altar as an offering. Animals appear at the window, mooing, barking and braying. The policeman tells Aaron that the cows are demanding extreme unction.

Aaron carries out a catechism with the servants on the definition of God. The last to answer asserts that Aaron is God. He does not deny this and forgives her sins, demanding that the others cleanse themselves by bathing in a fountain. A Greek pagan water sprite emerges and kisses Aaron and his spell is broken. The face of Madame Dina appears on the wall over the altar and condemns them all. 'From my breast you were fed and yet you have denied me.' The walls of the cathedral collapse and there is chaos. Darkness falls.

A fresh scene begins. Aaron is in a forest encircled by the Seven Daughters of the Wind, who sing a Shelleyesque lyric and then vanish. An ape enters and Aaron asks him what he should do next. The ape admonishes him for having no tail. 'You don't belong to our class at all.' The ape suggests that he might fly, but Aaron can find no feathers. Both are perplexed.

The shade of a woman appears. It is the servant whose sins were forgiven, now raised up like a Madonna except that she wears a crown of thorns and her hands carry Christ's stigmata. She vanishes and the face of Madame Dina reappears momentarily. Another apparition, which Aaron names Galatea, emerges. Aaron pursues and catches her, only to discover that she has a head identical to his own. He releases her, runs away and throws himself down on a rock. Madame Dina reappears briefly and then Aaron is surrounded by a host of his own doubles.

The sun rises and the kitchen maid enters accompanied by two men with angelic wings carrying a man-sized crib. She tucks him into this and, as the sun fades once more, sings a lullaby to him.

'The moon is dim. Instead of the mellow glow, a vague indeterminate radiance. The song and the light pass away together. Silence and darkness, as it was in the beginning.'

Evelyn never made it clear whether the source of this was a literal dream or whether it was a fantasy cast in the form of a dream. But certainly any significance the reader can derive from it is available only through a method of dream analysis. In our century the dream has undergone artistic investigation by Surrealists and scientific investigation by psychologists, yet it remains the most personal and untranslatable art-form. Few dreams survive translation into language, and fewer still permit even a fraction of their meaning to be conveyed to a second party.

When she wrote *Escapade* Evelyn, in common with a large section of American intelligentsia, accepted Freud as cartographer of the royal road to the unconscious. A Freudian reading of the dream might reveal something, but surely not as much as the fact that Evelyn referred to the passage as 'the beard chapter', when there is no mention of beards. A Jungian might draw attention to religious and mythological trappings, but to the average reader the episode communicates nothing except bewilderment. As an explanation of all and everything in the interior world of Evelyn Scott, its significance lies as an indicator of the author's immense egoism in offering such a personal parable to the public and expecting it to be understood.

7
Emergence of the
Mystery Woman

⸺⸻

EVELYN EXPLAINED to Upton Sinclair that she ended *Escapade* with the departure from Cercadinho because, when Cyril got the job with the International Ore Corporation, another phase of life began. Cyril bluffed his way into the post with the resourcefulness which carried him through many tight situations, but made a success of his new career. He was able to borrow enough money to dress his family in the fashion expected of him and settle them in a comfortable five-room company house in Villa Nova.

The European war which had caused the group to be stranded in Brazil was also the cause of their deliverance from Cercadinho. The treaty of Brest-Litovsk had closed Russian manganese sources to the Allies and there was a desperate search for alternative sources of supply. Cyril regarded the war as the inevitable result of a machine culture which subjected the individual to its service and saw ideology as the spiritual counterpart of mechanisation. But he was willing to subjugate himself to the machine efficiently in order to feed his family and, within several months, became office manager. A great deal of his time was spent travelling and he took to reading Plato and the New Testament, developing on the mystical intuitions he had felt at the ranch: 'Life, and the heart of man, are mystical. If a marriage completely blest by true love isn't a sacrament, and the last meal eaten with a loved one going off to war to give his life for you not a eucharist, then there is nothing in the universe above erectile tissue and gastric juice.'

He became a Christian by conviction, aware of the irony that his work enabled other Christians to kill one another. But then, he posited, he had not made the world, and the increasing need for manganese to satiate Christian blood-lust resulted in his promotion to director of eleven mines and finally to company manager for the state of Bahia.

The household had bounced back in social standing from *Yanqui sertanjeros* to utter respectability. On Independence Day the town band and school choir serenaded them with a barely recognisable version of 'The Star-Spangled Banner', and when they moved to São Salvador their acceptability was such that the Church of England vicar would call for tea. Mrs Dunn's sense of proprieties was restored.

It was from Bahia that Evelyn began to contribute work to American and European literary magazines. How she came across such small-circulation metropolitan journals as *Poetry*, *Others* and *The Egoist* in Brazil is a mystery, but the choice of these magazines for her début was fortuitous.

Others was a magazine for poets who were developing and extending Imagism. Between 1915 and 1919 it published Eliot, Mina Loy, William Carlos Williams, Ezra Pound, Richard Aldington, Marianne Moore, Carl Sandburg, Wallace Stevens, H. D. and Djuna Barnes. Two of Evelyn's poems appeared in the final issue. The magazine was edited by Alfred Kreymborg, an enthusiastic if not always discriminating modernist. William Carlos Williams called *Others* an 'ice-breaker', hampered by its lack of critical standards from being able to give a clear direction forward. Kreymborg's reputation as an editor took a severe drubbing when he published some incomprehensible verse by a group calling themselves the Spectricists.

After publication it was made known that the Spectricists were Witter Bynner and a group of friends. The poems had been a hoax. With some justification Kreymborg commented that the hoax was responsible for the best Bynner had written, but the damage was done. By contemporary standards the Spectricists seem as credible as much of the avant-garde published alongside them. Critical standards had collapsed in the rush to experimentalism and only an editor of genius could be sure that he was not rejecting the wave of the future. *Others* also played host to the Choric School, a group of poets who had the imprimatur of Ezra Pound. They never identified themselves as

hoaxers, but their incomprehensibility was as dense as the Spectricists'.

Harriet Monroe's *Poetry* was a more staid, discriminating
organ. Its editor possessed an uncanny instinct for work of
quality, and she was sufficiently well-endowed to pay both her
contributors and her printers. The London *Egoist* had begun life
as a feminist journal, the *New Freewoman*. It later broadened its
horizons to a stance of eccentric individualism and had the
fortune to acquire T. S. Eliot as editorial assistant. In the
September 1919 issue Evelyn published a poem, 'Woman',
alongside a section of *Ulysses* and the first part of Eliot's essay
'Tradition and the Individual Talent'. The final issue in
December contained the second part of Eliot's essay, a further
chapter of *Ulysses*, Williams' *Chicago* and Evelyn's critical essay,
'A Tardy Obeisance'.

This was an appreciation of George Douglas' novel *The House
with the Green Shutters* which had been published fifteen years
earlier and which was in danger of becoming a forgotten book.
Douglas' grim tragedy set in Puritan Scotland foreshadowed the
bleakness of Evelyn's early novels and in his celebration of
disease she saw a rare mastery of realism. Comparing Douglas
to Flaubert, Moore and Hardy, growing lyrical over his
remorseless anguish, her language resembles those critical
voices who were to speak favourably of her first novel, *The
Narrow House*.

In an immediate sense man knows nothing but himself and
the only life he can hand on is the experience of his own
being. Douglas has caught his Scotch environment, the part
of it so appropriated, in a bubble of glass as indestructible as
iron. I never read a book so particular in expression. He has
missed nothing at all of the peculiar acrid essence of his *locale*.
His use of the colloquial term in his own speeches is something unusual, for most authors esteem a conventionalised
vocabulary when the remark is not on one of their creature's
lips. But Douglas has accepted the most infinitesimal significance of his background. So strongly has he hated that he has
bared his breast and allowed the hideousness of these people
to be branded there, disfiguring himself that the world may
read it. He takes a disease and gives it back.

This celebration of pessimism chimed exactly with the mood of the time. Few who read it guessed that its author was a woman in her twenties who had been isolated from metropolitan intellectual currents for five years and whose experience before that was wholly provincial. To the literary world she was a curious enigma, and Lola Ridge would write of the time when Evelyn Scott was 'a mystery woman in far away Brazil', the most precocious and unlikely member of the emergent modern movement.

8

The Exiles Return

THE LAST TWO years in Brazil were comfortable ones. There was a single dramatic episode when Cyril was involved in an undercover operation against German-Brazilians who were involved in anti-Allied sabotage. An air of mystery hangs over this episode as recorded in *Life is too Short* and Evelyn later insisted that the whole episode was a concoction. If Cyril made the incident up, the story does not reflect well on his acumen as an agent for, having traced the two saboteurs, he returned to his hotel and took a bath. When one of the saboteurs entered the carelessly unlocked room, he was forced to defend himself, without revolver or trousers, against a knife attack. He was left with a foot-long knife wound in the stomach but the saboteurs were arrested and the incident may have been a contributory factor in the decision by the American Ambassador to grant Cyril and Evelyn emergency passports, under their assumed names, allowing their return home. Hostilities in Europe had ceased by this time and, as Evelyn observed, 'It is easier to get passports as the manager of an important corporation than as a nobody.'

The purpose of the return was for Evelyn to receive medical treatment. The company granted Cyril leave of absence and, sometime in mid-1919, the household set sail on the *Vauban* for New York, never to return.

When the boat docked, Cyril suggested to Mrs Dunn that she should return to her family in Clarksville. In spite of the friction of the last few years Mrs Dunn was unenthusiastic about this and eventually Cyril purchased a railway ticket, escorted her to the station and sent her home. For the remaining years of her life she was shuffled from one unwilling relative to another, dependent on her daughter for such minuscule financial independence as she had. In Clarksville she was remembered as being rather a forbidding figure in her late years. Her only daughter had become a subject of scandal, she had been deserted and divorced by her husband and was reliant on grudging charity for support. Only the memory of an aristocratic upbringing and its codes of propriety remained and she used these fully and imperiously to protect herself from further humiliation. Evelyn was to live constantly with the knowledge that at any moment the Clarksville relatives might tire of their charge and Mrs Dunn might be thrust wholly in her care.

Shortly after arrival, Cyril and Evelyn met Mr Dunn and his new wife, Melissa. Cyril berated him for the underhand trick of off-loading responsibility for Mrs Dunn on to him and the two men did not meet again. Evelyn fictionalised her relationship with her father during this period in an unpublished short story, 'Remarriage', in which Mr Dunn is portrayed as too beaten and confused to hold resentment, having instead taken refuge in drink. His new wife, a few years older than her stepdaughter, does not get on with her and the ill-feeling is reciprocated. The stepmother in the story recounts with pride her father's involvement in a lynching. She adheres to old Southern values and has little in common with her stepdaughter who feels that 'poor painters and half-starved writers were the salt of the earth'.

Mr Dunn gave some financial support to Evelyn but in 1926 ceased to reply to her letters. In later years Melissa became an arch-conspirator in the paranoid world which Evelyn constructed; a schemer who had turned her father against her and swindled her out of her inheritance. More probably Mr Dunn, whose correspondence from Evelyn consisted frequently of begging letters, decided that he would sever links with a painful past, rather as his daughter had done.

Cyril was summoned to the head office of the International Ore Corporation in Philadelphia while in New York and offered a post in Rio de Janeiro as chief representative in Brazil and Argentina. His salary would be doubled. Unfortunately the increased responsibility required him to be bonded and he could give no account of a business career prior to arrival in Brazil without revealing his true identity. Eventually the position was refused on the pretext of Evelyn's ill health. In New York she underwent an operation to correct the botched surgery which followed her childbirth, and she also needed considerable dental treatment.

She had visited New York only briefly during elopement and the shock of Manhattan after Brazil was expressed in a letter to Harriet Monroe, published in *Poetry*:

> It would take a long time to adjust oneself to this overpowering environment. In a sense the very democratic aspect of our institutions, when viewed at close range, gives me an impression of hopelessness from the individual's standpoint. Picturesque injustice may fire one to an equally colourful rebellion, but there is something 'boyg'-like (if I may coin the simile from Peer Gynt's experiences) in this negative quality. None of this is to decry Americanism, but simply to express a perhaps too emotional conviction of one of its necessary evils. Uniformity augments a meagre personality, but diminishes the impressiveness of a vivid one. So much of our education, especially along cultural lines, seems to content itself with admonitions as to what *not* to do.

She did not return and kiss the soil of her native land. Neither did many troops returning at the same time from the battlefields of Europe. It seemed that writers were pouring into Greenwich Village, each carrying the genesis of a first novel which recounted the agony of being a sensitive soul in a small Mid-Western town. A great moral and intellectual revulsion against received ideas of America began in the postwar years and lasted through most of the twenties. This was nothing new, but before there had always been Europe as an escape from 'a half-savage country, out of date'. Europe had culture, civilisation, history: everything missing from the land of commercialism and the fast buck, a land which demeaned its artists and whose people lived mean lives on a Main Street which ran coast to coast.

Van Wyck Brooks pointed out in *Days of the Phoenix* that the spectacle of Europe destroying itself in war showed that the Jamesian solution for the American artist was no longer feasible. Eliot and Pound were perhaps the last major writers to come to Europe with a view to assimilation. Yet, during the twenties, the

outflow of Americans to Paris was to create the enduring myth of
the 'lost generation'.

But these new expatriates differed from the old. Few who
congregated in the Dome or Rotonde sought to become Euro-
peans and, in exile, they wrote almost exclusively of America or of
Americans in exile. Paris was simply a backdrop with favourable
exchange rates and no prohibition, where the antics of the artistic
colony were looked upon with indulgence. 'Where else in the
world', marvelled William Carlos Williams, recalling his few
months in the city, 'could one feel the reticence, the freedom for
the individual, the willingness to permit such creatures as we
Americans, drunken, loud, often obscene, to exist in their city?'

The expatriates were only one wing of the artistic eruption of
the twenties. A number of artists, Williams among them, elected
to remain in America to create an authentic American art on
home ground. Both they and the expatriates addressed themselves largely to the solution of a great imponderable: what does it
mean to be an American?

In the struggle for an answer several tendencies emerged. A
critical wing, men such as Sinclair Lewis and Mencken, casti-
gated America as a land of Babbittry and stunted, broken lives;
wrote off tracts of the country as 'the Sahara of the Bozart' and
designated an entire class as 'the booboisie'. If they had a vision of
an ideal America, it was obscured by the mordancy of their
description of current reality, and their function was purgative
rather than prophetic. In *This was the Nightingale*, Ford Madox
Ford commented: 'The business of art is not to elevate but to
render. Those are the two schools of thought that have eternally
divided humanity, and no one in the end will ever know which will
win out.' But most renderers of America in the twenties saw only
hopelessness.

Many who felt the need for a redeeming vision congregated in a
loose group around the photographer Alfred Stieglitz, though the
grouping was amorphous and its members not uncritical of one
another. With *Port of New York: Essays on Fourteen American
Moderns*, Paul Rosenfeld emerged in 1924 as the critical champion of this tendency. In his opinion the work of the fourteen
artists and writers was so closely related as to form variations on a
single theme. 'For the first time, among these modern men and
women, I found myself in an America where it was good to be,' he

asserted. The group was anti-ideological, pro-American and much concerned with the need of the artist to come to terms with America and not seek European escape.

One of the prophets of the group, Waldo Frank, was mysteriously excluded from the survey. He had been the subject of a book-length study by Gorham Munson in the previous year in which Munson had commented on Rosenfeld's gushing and almost unreadable prose: 'Paul Rosenfeld; is there any justification for calling him a critic beyond the possession by him of a rich and muddy emotional equipment?' Even among its prophets, the house was divided.

Retrospectively Van Wyck Brooks felt deep reservations about the major prophet:

I had never felt at home in the petite chapelle either at '291' or the 'American Place'. It was Stieglitz's line that he who is not with us is against us, somewhat in the manner of Whitman fifty years before, obviously as a result of the feeling, which he shared with the great Walt, that he was involved in a losing battle. Whitman had talked about 'our crowd' as if not to be in it meant that you were not merely outside but hostile, and so it was with Stieglitz also. If you could not be his disciple and could not be his enemy, you had to maintain in his presence a certain aloofness.

A redeeming sense of humour was absent from their activities and pronouncements, which combined high seriousness and inflated self-importance. Lee Simonson, a theatrical member of the group, informed Van Wyck Brooks: 'We are all prophets, Puritans like you and Hebrews like Waldo and myself. But the practice of letters is a cause, and it will have to be kept one. Or made one again.'

Between the prophetic heirs to Whitman's mantle and the renderers of a despoiled America, a heterogeneous group of artists struggled with their own visions. In 1919 the European exodus had not begun and Greenwich Village was a crucible to which many of those who were to shape American art in the twenties had been drawn. It was the most exciting place in the world for a writer to be, and it was here, after five years in an alien culture, that Cyril and Evelyn made their home for the next two years.

9

Village Voices - *1*

THE SCOTTS' STATUS as mysterious distant contributors to literary magazines meant that they were not alone in New York for long. They moved into the apartment of Lewis and Mary Gannett, an influential and well-connected couple in the New York book world, both of whom reviewed for solidly established magazines. Lewis Gannett was at that time on the editorial staff of *The Nation*. The atmosphere at their Barrow Street apartment, where casual visitors included John Cowper Powys, Frank Harris, Sinclair Lewis, Marianne Moore, Sherwood Anderson, John Dos Passos and Mark Van Doren, was conducive to the Scotts' developing ambition to become writers. Living expenses augmented by heavy medical bills meant that there was soon a money problem, which eased when the ever resourceful Cyril found a job as a reporter on a trade woman's wear daily, the *Daily Garment News*. The former medical missionary, college dean, baggage carrier, Brazilian rancher and mining engineer entered on a new, equally unlikely career. Though he had no newspaper experience he seems to have been efficient for, within three months, he was made departmental editor.

Though Evelyn's health was poor she wrote a great deal of verse and began to review in a serious way for *The Dial*, then edited by Schofield Thayer. *The Dial* was the voice of mainstream modernism and one of the few advanced periodicals which paid its contributors, albeit at a cent a word. The *Little Review*, a more erratic and extreme publication, had gained celebrity when it took over serialisation of *Ulysses* from *The Egoist*. However, it could not afford to pay its contributors and money, and how to get it, preoccupied the Scotts a great deal at this time. *Broom*, the other major vehicle of New York literary experiment, could not even afford to pay its editors.

Evelyn's time with *The Dial* was productive but short-lived. She contributed poems, book reviews and several lengthy critical articles, the most important of which, 'A Contemporary of the Future', was the first examination in depth of the work of James Joyce to appear in America. It was not uncritical and gave excessive praise to Joyce's rather ordinary play, *Exiles*, but it also included comment on those parts of *Ulysses* which had been serialised in magazines. It was sufficiently laudatory to prompt a brief thank-you note from Joyce himself.

Evelyn's early championship of Joyce did not stop here. When she became involved with the Provincetown Players she wrote to Joyce and secured his permission for the first American performance of *Exiles*, which that company gave. *Ulysses* became a *cause célèbre* when John Sumner of the Society for the Suppression of Vice halted its serialisation in the *Little Review*, and Evelyn went to Sumner's office to register her disapproval in person. Unsurprisingly her appearance failed to stop the prosecution. Like Margaret Anderson, co-editor of the *Little Review*, Evelyn found Sumner not quite a worthy opponent, but at least a person worthy of consideration. In an unpublished short story, 'A Strong Man', she fictionalised him as having 'the thin courage of an unacknowledged servitor' who felt toward the books he condemned 'a faint sweet terror of their lasciviousness'. She thought that the whole matter of art bewildered him.

She also reviewed Lawrence's *Women in Love* and *The Lost Girl* for *The Dial* in a piece whose title, 'A Philosopher of the Erotic', oddly prefigures his later biographical designation as 'The Priest of Love'. The review was critical but not unsympathetic, and took Lawrence's artistic role seriously enough. Of *Women in Love* she observed that 'having written it, Lawrence might turn philosopher or priest. It is the last word of his living truth. Anything further in this nature would be mere exposition. The book might as well be the last word of an age in revolt against the intellectualism to which it has been betrayed; an after-war world hectically clutching at immediacy; a world in which Parnassianism has brought forth the dadaists.' Lawrence did not find the review 'very sensible', but evidently bore no ill will. It was, after all, one of the few serious notices to appear in America.

The routine of literary life was interrupted when young Creighton contracted, in rapid succession, bronchitis, influenza, measles, a mastoid ear and whooping cough. An infancy in the tropics left him ill-prepared for the rigours of a New York winter. A doctor advised recuperation in the country and Cyril was granted two weeks' leave from his job to take care of him. Evelyn promptly fell ill on arrival at their retreat and the two weeks had to be extended to three. At the end of the third week Cyril received a letter informing him that he was fired, because a newspaper 'was like a theatrical company or a train, and no matter what happened, must go on with all on board'. Evelyn would recall that her vengeful nature was satisfied when the editor was arraigned on a charge of neglecting his own children, was deserted by his wife and subsequently died of delirium tremens in a hospital.

The sacking meant that debts mounted once more until Cyril began a job as researcher with the Guarantee Trust Company. Office work was uncongenial but it was to keep the family alive for a year. Jig was boarded out by a charitable trust to an old lady in upstate New York where he spent several months safe from the Manhattan climate, tranquillised by opiated cough syrup.

Cyril was disturbed by the moral rather than meteorological climate of the village. His autobiography shows that he was no prude, but he was unimpressed by the mores of Bohemianism and by Evelyn's adoption of them with enthusiasm. At fifty he was considerably older than the average Villager and had never experienced life in this milieu before, most of his adulthood having been spent either beyond civilisation or in staid professional circles. Unlike many around him he had family responsibilities which meant that he had to endure a series of tedious jobs. 'Bohemianism is like measles: it is something you should get over young,' he stated sourly. But he was no longer young, and became increasingly unsympathetic to their new circle of friends. He regarded Bohemia as a refuge for those suffering from parental interference, a state which those with talent or something to say would soon outgrow. The rest, of necessity the majority, survived by a sort of 'spiritual nudism', and making a great fetish from their own sensitivity. He tired of endless outpourings and self-deprecations, and the leech-like activities of those who sought a solution to their problems by using him as a confession box. He remarked that, on alcoholic and sexual indulgence, Bohemia no longer had the edge over country clubs and restricted residential circles. It was the continuous histrionics he could not stand.

Foremost among the matters on which *Life is too Short* is circumspect are the men who became Evelyn's lovers. It became apparent shortly after arrival in New York that she regarded their common-law marriage as an open arrangement. During 1920 she had two intense affairs with other men and committed a number of minor infidelities, with the result that by summer the couple had decided to separate. Evelyn had embraced everything about Bohemia which he found distasteful and his description of her activities has a venom suggesting that he was deeply wounded by them:

> Some of the people we knew in the Village were fine, others were only vicious little cowards, sadists and debauchees. But to her, the only mark of 'goodness' was complete lack of reticence. This she called 'honesty'; but it was simply more of her anachronistic rebellion against a convention that was no longer a problem in her life. So, quarrelling with most of the friends she and I had made together, she gradually replaced them with others I could not stomach. With neither malice nor pity she strove to get into the entrails of people's minds, to destroy what she termed 'hypocrisies' but which were the person's self – happy when shattering something, and breaking completely with whoever objected.
>
> It wasn't only this rapidly growing emotional nihilism, or even her absolute lack of reserve; but when the latter began to include me I objected. She was breaking down everything in sight, including herself; and I didn't propose to be included.

According to *Life is too Short* the couple permanently separated at this point. However, this is one of the elisions of truth that characterise the book; they in fact stayed together until 1925, sharing the same house if not always the same bed. He remained the dominant influence on her development and the man to whom she turned when crisis loomed. They were to remain deeply involved until the mid-thirties, but as passionate friends rather than lovers.

Though Evelyn told Upton Sinclair that Cyril suffered a nervous breakdown at this time, such anguish as he felt is concealed in the autobiography. Nor is the name mentioned of the man who supplanted Cyril after the separation: the brilliant but egoistic novelist and critic, Waldo Frank.

10
The Ego and His Own

WALDO FRANK is barely remembered today; if at all, he is known as a friend of Hart Crane, for whose posthumous collected poems he wrote an introduction. He underwent the painful experience of watching his star fade from the literary firmament and his old friend Lewis Mumford was to observe that after the Second World War he became too obscure to be worth attacking.

In many ways he was a male counterpart of Evelyn and there were numerous similarities and polarities in their respective careers. He too was an egoist who saw his role both as novelist and social redeemer. He led a sexually adventurous life, which included three marriages and numerous affairs and he too opposed the reduction of the individual by machine culture. Though Evelyn disclaimed Frank's influence, there are similarities of style and manner in the early fiction of both writers. In the thirties, both would write semi-autobiographical novels, *Eva Gay* and *The Death and Birth of David Markand* which were, to some extent, admissions of failure. Later they would involve themselves on opposing sides with the political controversies of that decade. In spite of this, they were temperamentally outsiders who shared a tendency toward mysticism of a diffuse and ill-defined sort. Both, in essence and often in declared belief, were anarchists.

While Evelyn was the last scion of an aristocratic line, Frank was the child of a moderately wealthy New York Jewish family. He retained a strong sense of Jewish identity, though his upbringing had been secular, and his dark, intense appearance in youth meant that he could easily pass as a Latin. At one time he masqueraded for several months as a Negro in the South.

His early career was physically and intellectually precocious. In the memoir he wrote in old age he revealed that the unifying myth dominating his life was an image of himself as an adolescent lying naked in the bath contemplating his erect penis from which the known world radiated. This phallocentric conception he named Waldea and it was to inform all his later activities.

When he entered Yale University in 1907, a book was published in translation which seemingly validated his intuitions. *The Ego and His Own* was the only volume written by Max Stirner, a contemporary and associate of Marx. It has been called 'the most revolutionary book ever written', and when Marx criticised his philosophical rivals among the Young Hegelians in *The German Ideology*, much space was devoted to a choleric attack on Stirner. Marx might well have felt insecure since in 1845 Engels had written to him confessing that he had been temporarily converted to Stirner's philosophy.

Stirnerian egoism is a developed position and more than a Thelemic injunction of 'Do what thou wilt'. Stirner asserted that individual desire and will took precedence over social structures and obligations, and laid emphasis on the creative force of the free individual within society. The ideal society was one of healthy, competing, conscious egoists. Frank had intuitively grasped this in his myth of Waldea and the book simply validated what he already knew.

From Yale his career was effortlessly brilliant and he gravitated, via journalism, to New York where he became involved in *Seven Arts* magazine, the first journal to express an authentic modernist American voice. Yet his sense of outsiderdom persisted and significantly his first novel was called *The Unwelcome Man*. In 1919 he published *Our America*, a visionary, Whitmanic book which addressed itself to the question of 'What does it mean to be an American?' and seemed to find an answer in the activities of the Stieglitz group.

Lewis Mumford suggested that many of Frank's problems resulted from an immense ego encountering too few initial setbacks. He was affluent, intellectually brilliant and before thirty had become a power in the New York literary world. He had a greater name to come, it was generally felt, though many privately deplored his egoism. In the early seventies Mumford suggested that 'many of Frank's convictions and much of his conduct could not be interpreted fully until the same traits – the same inordinate expectancies, the same demand for instant compliance – were magnified in the imperious conduct of the younger generation today'. In the action of the demonstrator who scrawled the Jim Morrison line 'We want the world and we want it now' on the walls of the London School of Economics in 1968, Mumford saw, to his apparent regret, an amplification of the spirit which had animated Frank half a century earlier; an amplification made possible by the onset of mass affluence.

The egoism of Evelyn Scott and Waldo Frank may well have been at their respective dizzying heights when they met in 1920. The affair was probably short-lived as a physical liaison but from it a quarrelsome friendship developed which continued for many years. Its practical consequences were the separation from Cyril, who deeply detested Frank, and a weakening of Frank's marriage with progressive educator Margaret Naumburg, who divorced him after numerous infidelities in 1925.

Through the friendship, Evelyn was drawn to the fringes of the Stieglitz group and, though she respected many of them, she was unimpressed by their pious talk of 'redeeming America'. She found Frank's pretensions alternatively amusing and irritating, and caricatured him as the vain, self-deluded artist, Dudley Allen, in her novel *Narcissus*. Apart from physical passion, there was an idealised side to the affair and Frank wrote execrable free verse about Evelyn filled with images of oriental conceit: 'Your brow is the scarf/of knowing, flung/about the depths of God.'

Evelyn confessed to Lola Ridge that she was unsure how he would react to her caricature in *Narcissus*. When he read the novel it is likely that his vanity was such that he did not see himself, for he simply commented: 'Any person who does not recognise the significance of *Narcissus* in modern prose art is unqualified, that is all.' But he added the proviso, 'The question of the pleasurability of the material you have employed is another matter.' In a later letter he compared the book's appearance to that of a foetus when a human was expected.

Frank praised both Cyril and Evelyn as novelists in the early twenties, though Evelyn felt that she was being damned with faint

praise and treated as a protégé. The methods of Frank's 1920
novel *The Dark Mother* foreshadow in a more extreme form
Evelyn's early excursions in prose, and it is clear that he was, for a
time, her main influence:

> Blackness ... ultimate texture of all colors ... light. A world of
> infinite color, infinite flesh: himself within the world, himself
> carried within it, through it. Himself of the breakless tissue of
> the world. Flesh of sweet smells, sweet odors, sweet fluids.
> Flesh altogether and altogether about him. He altogether
> touching all Flesh – and ALL. David knew through his shut
> eyes, walking the world, how he was carried within a world of
> ceaseless substance: how he was substance within it: how his
> moving and knowing through Flesh was Spirit ... He walked –
> he worked – he ate. He had a woman's body, he earned the
> bread of a man, he held the love of a friend. Flesh, all, and his
> moving through Flesh, his moving through infinite immersion
> through the Night, through the World of Flesh – Spirit and
> Dawn ...

The stance and technique are familiar now, though in 1920
they were not. Frank's prose was a form of solipsistic utterance
which has since become almost a tradition in the self-styled
avant-garde. The reader is in a world without characterisation, in
which physical phenomena, a term including everything except
the observing 'I', assumes greater importance than persons or
narrative. It is a dull world, and a blind alley down which literature
might have turned but mercifully did not. In 1920 the future of
literature was not so clear. Even Frank came to look on *The Dark
Mother* as a failure, though he was incensed on publication by
Paul Rosenfeld's critical review in *The Dial*, which he wrongly
ascribed to jealousy. Evelyn also reviewed the book, concluding:
'Economy is an aesthetic law. Both in method and material, Mr
Frank is riotously wasteful.'

As a novelist Frank was an interesting failure but as critic and
social commentator he is not so easily dismissed. During the
twenties he became fascinated by Hispanic culture and this
interest culminated in his 1931 book *American Hispania* which
postulated a new sense of the American continent including
North and South. Interest in Latin America continued until the

early sixties when he visited Fidel Castro and was active on the Fair Play for Cuba Committee. Nowadays his reputation is far higher in the Hispanic world than in his native land.

His memoir written in the final years of obscurity addressed the question whether his life's work had been a failure. As a forgotten man it was a question he was entitled to ask and, with uncharacteristic humility, he partly blamed his downfall on egoism. Neither in this book nor in the voluminous journals which he habitually kept is the name of Evelyn Scott mentioned. His self-image as a mythic being was a constant source of friction in relations with women: 'My sex partner had to play a conscious drama of fusion and of union with my idea. Of course, this caused trouble. It was a burden for the woman to find her body exalted as an allegory and ignored as a fact. If they are honest with themselves, women do not like it. My second wife, for instance, who was a blue-eyed, golden-haired Yankee from New Hampshire found that her "accepting" me meant (to me) Anglo-America's acceptance of the dark Mediterranean "outsider".'

The sense of being an outsider lay at the root of his egoism: 'I've always felt myself an *outsider* – yearning, struggling to *get in. Into* my own home, *into* N.Y. of the people, *into* France (later Spain), *into* literary America (7 Arts, Our America and the 1920s), *into* the Revolution (the People). I've never succeeded – whence the growing stress and importance of "*into* the Cosmos".'

The pinnacle of these struggles to belong came in the thirties when he came to believe that, by force of his own will, he could change the direction of American communism. He never joined the Party but collaborated through front organisations and Soviet-sponsored Cultural Congresses sufficiently to become identified with its aims. The *Memoirs* consider why a person of his anarchist temperament should have been drawn to this quasi-militarist organisation and retrospectively assert that his activities were geared to a transformation of Party policy to a new, Waldean communism which he termed 'integral communism'. This was a revolution of the whole man which he termed 'the deep revolution' and it would liberate the masses both spiritually and economically.

The folly of expounding these ideas to solid unimaginative Party functionaries never occurred to him. The Party was glad to use him since its cultural front was well-stocked with critics but

short on actual artists. So Frank made his prophetic utterances
which the functionaries ignored, content to have him adorn their
platform. Theodore Dreiser had a similar on/off relationship
with communism, but proved to be even less reliable than Frank,
whose utility ended abruptly after the 1936 show trials when he
proposed an international tribunal to examine the question of
Trotsky's guilt. In the next issue of the *Daily Worker*, party leader
Earl Browder attacked Frank as a fool, weakling and hopeless
bourgeois.

Frank travelled to Mexico City to meet Trotsky and found him
and his wife to be 'a homely elderly pair, very Jewish, very
bourgeois'. Smiling all the while, Trotsky accused him of colla-
borating with the Stalinists then gave a two-and-a-half-hour
analysis of current events in Soviet Russia. When Frank left he
was no clearer regarding Trotsky's guilt or innocence, but felt he
had met a fanatic who would expend any life willingly in order that
the revolution should continue on the correct course.

The *Memoirs* blame much of Frank's lapse into obscurity on his
espousal of communism. After 1936 he was regarded as a
Trotskyist, a peculiarly friendless position which meant that he
could be shot at by both sides with impunity. His search for a
community had failed again and he began increasingly to interest
himself in various forms of mysticism. Involvement with Latin
America continued and his last book in 1961 was a paean to
Castro's Cuba, *The Prophetic Island*. Though he admired the
Cuban Revolution, after meeting Castro he privately confessed to
finding in him the same fanaticism he had discerned in Trotsky.

Revolutions are not made by self-regarding egoists with a
yearning for visionary leadership and the posthumously
published *Memoirs* admit that many of his activities had been
quixotic tilting at windmills. Yet his vision of America Hispania
remains a solid one, and one likely to grow in importance with the
numerical rise of the Hispanic community within the United
States and the increasing emphasis in American foreign policy on
Latin American affairs. The cause of his failure was beyond his
control and lay in the never realised desire to escape the confines
of Waldea, the self-absorbed adolescent contemplating his body
in the bath: the prison of the ego and his own.

11

Village Voices - 2

EVELYN'S DÉBUT volume was a book of verse, *Precipitations*, published by Nicholas L. Brown in 1920. It excited much favourable comment and H. L. Mencken gave it his stamp of approval, which counted for a lot. Lola Ridge gave a complimentary review in *Poetry* and William Carlos Williams wrote privately: 'You are the only real female poet that can write anything at all to my way of thinking – except H.D.' But he added the telling qualification, 'And you haven't written it yet . . . '

Precipitations was a book of promise, rather than fully fledged talent. What gave it distinction was the way in which the world was suffused with, for its time, a violent female eroticism:

Summer Night

The bloated moon
Has sickly leaves glistening against her
Like flies on a fat white face.

The thick-witted drunkard on the park bench
Touches a young girl's breast
That throbs with its own ruthless and stupid delight.
The new-born child crawls in his mother's filth.
Life, the sleepwalker
Lifts toward the skies
An immense gesture of indecency.

Though *Precipitations* was a promising start, Evelyn lacked either the will or the technical ability to develop on it. As her career as a novelist evolved she continued to write verse but issued only one further volume. *The Winter Alone* was published in 1930 on the strength of the commercial and critical success of *The Wave*, but showed little advance on the work of a decade earlier. The book was critically savaged by Dudley Fitts in *Poetry*, who held it up as an example of what was wrong with much American verse.

In 1920 she received much help and encouragement from William Carlos Williams, whom she had approached in the previous year with a sheaf of poems asking for his comments. Williams' *Autobiography* states that he was a highly sexual man and Evelyn soon shifted roles from disciple to lover. Photographs reveal her to have been a considerable beauty whose most striking feature was her huge, luminous eyes. She was in her late twenties and possessed a talent which Williams felt would mature with careful nurturing.

The affair developed in the early months of 1920. Williams was highly regarded by many Villagers for, though he lived the life of a weekend Bohemian, he was a doctor ministering to a working-class practice, and a highly respected poet. It was his aim to forge a genuinely American poetic idiom and, in this, he was Whitman's true heir.

He was something of a *naif* at this time of his life. He lived, as he would until death, in a house in Rutherford, New Jersey, with his wife Flossie. Though he had seen something of Europe in company with Ezra Pound, he had decided it was not for him. The Armory show of 1913, which sprang European modernism on an unsuspecting American public, had come as a revelation, but he was coolly snubbed by its star Marcel Duchamp at a New York party. Constrained by responsibilities, the freedom of the Village excited him and his trips between Rutherford and New York became more frequent and his motive more openly carnal.

Williams' *Autobiography* is circumspect about names and places and Evelyn is mentioned only in passing. The affair he could not suppress, which was apparently never consummated, was his involvement with the Baroness Else von Freytag-Loringhoven. With the encouragement of Duchamp she was the purest expression of Zurich Dada to be found in New York; a woman with an impossibly chequered past given to walking the streets with a coal scuttle on her head or postage stamps dotted over her face. She lived in an apartment of indescribable squalor and her rapaciousness was such that Wallace Stevens would not venture below Fourteenth Street for fear of encountering her. She too was highly sexual and pursued Williams until he admitted in a moment of weakness that he loved her. He was fond of her and throughout his life was to be drawn to women, not necessarily beautiful ones, who bore the marks of a wealth of experience. A watershed in their friendship came when the Baroness suggested that their love should be cemented by her giving him syphilis, and from here on things took a downhill course. The Baroness proved tenacious and pursued Williams to Rutherford where she made highly embarrassing scenes for the town doctor with a secret life elsewhere. He was forced to have her arrested and later gave her money to leave the country. Some years later her story came to a tragic end when she was gassed by a casual pick-up in a hotel room.

The Baroness was the cause of a high-flown literary quarrel between Evelyn and Jane Heap, an editor of the *Little Review*. The magazine fervently espoused modernism and experimentation in a not too discriminatory way and its editors had taken the Baroness under their wing. They published one of her prose-poems early in 1920 titled *Mineself – Minesoul – and – mine – Cast Iron Lover*. The poem was not strictly Dadaist since it possessed a schizophrenic logic, and, for all her modernism, the author retained old English usages of conventional poetic diction. However the result was startling enough:

Yea – mine soul – and he brushes and combeth it – he maketh it shining and glistening around his head – and he is vain about it – but alas – mine soul – his hair is without sense – his hair does not live – not GOLDEN animal – he is gilded animal only – mine soul! His vanity is without sense – it is the vanity of one who has little and who weareth a treasure meaningless! O – mine soul – THAT soulless beauty maketh me sad.

The poem continues in similar vein over several pages, reaching a climax marked by the entry of a golden toad. The golden toad finally dreams itself to be a bee:

MINE PROUD SOUL – is he crippled – DISGUISED TO
HIMSELF ONLY? NOR is he disguised to thine body – nor –
wise patient soul – to THEE!
WILL PUT HIM ON CENTER OF CRIMSON THRONE –
SHALL SQUAT AND BASK – – – OR PERISH AND BURN!
THINE BODY AND THOU – MINE SOUL – WE DO NOT
LIKE CRIPPLES! UPRIGHT WE STAND – – – SLANDER WE
FLARE – – – THINE BODY AND THOU – MINE SOUL – –
– HISSING! –
THUS – MINE SOUL – IS MINE SONG TO THEE – – –
THUS ITS END.

This was too much even for so dedicated a modernist as Lola
Ridge who wrote to the magazine protesting at 'this retching
assault on Art'. The following issue contained a letter by Evelyn
who had picked up on Jane Heap's comment that the poem was
an example of the art of madness. Evelyn declared herself broadly
in favour and commented: 'Else von Freytag-Loringhoven is to
me the naked oriental making solemn gestures of indecency in the
naked sex dance of her religion. Her ecstasy, to my way of
thinking, is one of the properties of art.'

This guarded defence did not impress Jane Heap who
countered that the Baroness had chosen madness as a permanent
state and was not merely making a foray into it. The next issue saw
a further rejoinder from Evelyn which was convoluted to the point
of near-incomprehensibility but said in essence that madness was
not a matter of choice and that the Baroness was, in fact, mad.
Jane Heap replied alleging that 'the lady doth protest too much'
and Else von Freytag-Loringhoven joined the argument on the
side of Jane Heap with a plea that the custom of Fasching be
incorporated into American life. Undeterred, Evelyn wrote in the
next issue that, though she appreciated the poem to a limited
extent, it was a limited creation since its author 'was far too
inspired to think'. The argument on both sides was becoming
obfuscatory and Jane Heap wisely withdrew with this final judgement on Evelyn: 'I feel that I have been permitted a glimpse of
the gentle mystic soul of an adding machine.'

The Baroness was a near neighbour and Evelyn would have
met her on many occasions. Whatever qualms she may have had
about her artistic direction, she admired her spirit and celebrated

her in a characteristically impenetrable imagist poem. 'Amy' is presumably Amy Lowell, the red-headed plutocratic promulgator of Imagism; a scarcely less baroque figure than the Baroness herself:

> *Portrait of Two Poetesses*
>
> *1. Baroness*
> Thick tree with open crotch
> in the air and complaining branches.
>
> *2. Amy*
> Blue sky in spittle
> embellishes sidewalk.

During these years Evelyn could be almost as disconcerting as the Baroness. When Margaret Anderson of the *Little Review* recalled a sometime lover in her memoirs she remarked: 'Dick and I talked ideas. Of course we talked monstrously – rather like Oswald Spengler or Evelyn Scott. But this curse can be gradually overcome.'

This coupling of Spengler and Scott is not so odd as might appear, as much of Evelyn's prose in the early twenties had a tendency to abstraction which made it difficult to understand. She sent such a piece, 'The Psychology of Renunciation', to Williams with a plea that he find a publisher for it; a plea which he seems to have wisely ignored:

> The self and the not-self being two phases of a single recognition are corroborative, one of the other, in intensity. God is the name we give to the not-self, thus by the synthetic trick which logic has given to language, veiling the chaotic features of our opposed ideal so that we may surrender ourselves to it on a practical basis. The small soul has a small God and finds it no trouble to carry Him about. The legend of Christopher or the Christ bearer, might be a parable of intensifying consciousness.

As Margaret Anderson suggested, fortunately the curse can be overcome. Evelyn experimented with almost every literary genre but her ventures in philosophy were probably the least successful.

The affair with Williams had probably reached a peak of intensity in May 1920 when Williams wrote her a high-flown incoherent letter which ran over four foolscap pages. He had involvements with other women and it is hard to gauge what emotional reality lay behind his protestations. On the face of it his statements seem sincere enough:

> No one could tolerate me for a moment if I behaved with all the stops open. Can no one understand that I am a king? That I am a baby who is always right? [...] Why do I write the things I do instead of continually spilling a waterfall of love songs? It is because I am harassed by humanity instead of welcomed by human beings [...] Nothing can blot out the terrible hopelessness that obsesses me day and night as to the futility of everything that is [...] Fear is my guiding star.
>
> Do you like this sort of love letter? Perhaps I am climbing to your balcony. It has not been necessary to climb though, so why pretend [...] Why do I keep up my pretences? Why do I not say I love you?

The letter is signed 'Bill'. None of Evelyn's letters to Williams has survived, though the frequency of references to the affair in her future correspondence suggests that, for her, the involvement was deeper than others of this time. Certainly within a year of this letter relations had considerably cooled. Possibly Williams found her intensity overwhelming and her predilection for 'telling the truth' as she saw it rather unnerving. Another factor may have been the appearance of a 'coldly intense' man called Robert McAlmon, who had been a life model at Cooper Union Art School before being taken up by the painter Marsden Hartley. Hartley was favoured by the Stieglitz group and was a friend of Williams; 'everybody's grandfather', Williams would call him, though threads of incestuous desire were shot through the grandpatriality. Hartley was fundamentally attracted to his own sex, hence the appeal of the sexually ambiguous McAlmon. Evelyn found a lifelong enemy in McAlmon whom she would later call her 'bête noire', but between him and Williams a friendship verging on love sprung up. McAlmon had been a drifter and adventurer but found a niche in the Village as a writer. He also began to publish others, and he and Williams founded

Contact Editions together. Fate appeared to smile on him when he was invited by a young woman writer called Bryher to enter into a *mariage blanc* so that she might continue to travel without parental opposition. Her parents were the Ellermans, reputedly the richest family in England, and the drifter seemed to have fallen squarely on his feet. The loveless pretence was to contribute to Mc-Almon's decline, though the money he received during the marriage and after the divorce settlement funded a good deal of publishing and social activity among the 'lost generation' expatriates. Shortly after the marriage McAlmon moved his wife and *Contact Editions* to Paris where he became a pivot of the growing Anglophone literary scene.

The break in the relationship with Williams would seem to have been on Evelyn's part. She borrowed a hundred and fifty dollars from him to tide her over a financial crisis, but the friendship could not survive his condemnation of her play *Love*. This was mounted by the Provincetown Players between February 28 and March 13, 1921 and a week after the play closed Evelyn received a brief note impersonally signed W. C. Williams in which he panned the play as 'impossible'. Others had liked it; Van Wyck Brooks had written ecstatically about it. Evelyn was never receptive to negative criticism of her work; doubtless a counterblast followed to which Williams replied on May 23, 1921. His poor opinion of the play had not lessened – 'the characters stumble on the stage without reason and off again still without reason' – but he did pay it the compliment of comparing it with Russian drama. In what was his last recorded communication with her, he added:

Don't ask to be forgiven for what I say nor am I much interested in hearing of the one fifty – which I wish you would please forget permanently. If it did you a service, I am glad. It is more, apparently, than I can do in person.

Yours, Bill.

12
Of Love, *and*
Other Things

THE IRONICALLY titled *Love* was written in Brazil and was little more than a piece of juvenilia. Though the reputation of the Provincetown Players was high, their production did not set the New York theatre world alight. Most critics commented on the poor acting and of the play itself the anonymous reviewer in *Theatre Magazine* stated: 'It is difficult to determine whether a play is good or bad, when it is badly presented.' The manuscript draft of the play confirms Williams' strictures, except that the shade of Ibsen rather than the Russians predominates.

Claude Mayfield is a writer/critic who has taken a younger second wife, Carroll Lamont. He has a son by his first marriage called Robert, who is six years younger than Carroll. Claude Mayfield's mother is holding a birthday party in her house, where the drama unfolds over a period of several hours. A pall of Strindbergian claustrophobia hangs over the gathering, and Mrs Mayfield emerges as the domineering mother figure recurrent in Evelyn's work. Carroll on the other hand is a liberated modern divorcee and clearly the object of the author's sympathy. To escape the unpleasant atmosphere in the house Robert decides to walk along the beach, and Carroll joins him.

In the second act Mrs Mayfield hints to Claude that relations between Carroll and her stepson are less than innocent. She is right. When they return it is clear that Robert is very drawn to Carroll, who confesses to a sexually delinquent past: 'I think I was seduced when I was fifteen, or I seduced the boy, I don't remember which. He was about your age. I've been going round and round in a circle ever since. Yes. It's just like I said – all the wells poisoned. You have to drink – .'

They kiss at Carroll's instigation. Later Claude and Mrs Mayfield join them and there is an unpleasant scene as their growing fondness becomes apparent.

The final act is a complexity of coming and going which ends with Robert trying to prevent Carroll from leaving the room, as he suspects she plans to commit suicide. He says he will kill himself too, if she does. Just then there is a pistol shot offstage. Claude has shot himself in the study.

In performance this may have been less melodramatic than synopsis suggests, but it is a far from great play. Its main interest lies in Evelyn's sympathy for Carroll, beside whom the other characters except Mrs Mayfield are pale and one-dimensional. The figure of Carroll Lamont is the first appearance of the 'Evelyn Scott woman', who was to recur as Julia in *Narcissus* and *The Golden Door* and more transparently in the title character of *Eva Gay*. It is tempting to identify her with her creator. She demands the right to express her sexuality on equal terms with men, without refuge to coquetry and without reference to the bonds of marriage. She resents her dependence on men but is unable to break free from it. She rejects her socially defined role but is an individual rebel, not part of a broad-based movement for change. Her men are often shadowy figures whose sexual attractiveness is not elaborated on. They are either older men with whom her relations are near-filial, or weak, confused men of her own age toward whom she is quasi-maternal. And she is always conscious of the gulf between her desires and what society expects of her. The heroine of an unpublished story, 'Lady Author', is struggling in a sanatorium for a sense of identity, oppressed by the fame of her father and her husband. She observes: 'For the millionth time, the indignity of being a woman and being bound to please overcame her.' And writing of sexual relations in Algeria Evelyn noted that women in America were allowed freedom with the proviso that 'self-expression *must* be idealistic, non-creative, social and therefore negative. There must be no recognition of beauty unfolding in the experience of flesh.'

Though she found closeness to women difficult, in New York Evelyn met a woman who was to be her dearest friend for the next two decades. Lola Ridge was older than Evelyn and semi-invalid,

facts which removed the stumbling blocks of sexual tension which
felled several friendships. Her poetry is now unread though her
name lives in many memoirs of interwar New York and most
American literary figures at some time mounted the stairs to her
tiny apartment at 7 East Fourteenth Street. Everyone met at
Lola's, 'that Vestal of the Arts, a devout believer in the humanity
of letters', as Williams recalled her.

She was born in Ireland in 1873 and reached America, after a
period in Australia, in 1907. She had a variety of jobs but by the
time she met Evelyn ill-health debarred her from anything
strenuous. In New York she had become an anarchist follower of
Emma Goldman and had contributed to her magazine, *Mother
Earth*. She later worked on the editorial staff of *Others* where she
first encountered the verse of 'a mystery woman in far off Brazil'.
When *Others* folded she began to work for *Broom*. Cyril remembered her as the only pure Romantic he knew and though he
admired her poetry he felt her Bohemianism in the old French
tradition was her greatest achievement. She was charismatic, and
Evelyn was not alone in falling under her spell. Few left her salon
with anything but good words for their hostess. In a subtle way her
influence on American letters was greater than many polemicists
and clique leaders for, by virtue of her radiant, dedicated spirit,
she made things happen.

When Cyril and Evelyn met Lola, they still planned to return to
Brazil after Evelyn had received medical treatment. Lola capti-
vated them to such a degree that Evelyn suggested that they take
her with them to Rio where her health might improve. For Evelyn
it was an encounter which changed her view of womanhood and
in Lola Ridge she discovered a female counterpart to Cyril: a
woman who was part passionate friend and part exemplar:

Dear Lola (may I call you that now?),
    Do you know what I have been thinking ever since yesterday?
Of course you don't. I was thinking that if I had known there
was somebody like you in the world a few years ago, some of my
conclusions about the universe would have been modified and
I would have been a good deal happier. When I was a lot more
of a kid I wanted a woman friend tremendously, but the
mystical kind of idea I had of a bond which would be a
recognition of a common defeat was something I had hardly

#

articulated and nobody else understood – and of course I never found the woman. Then I thought I would rather have a daughter than anything else. I had a son instead and I am glad, for the other would have been too cruel a luxury. My experience with women has always led me to a deeper conviction that they are too thoroughly without faith (due to several centuries of experience) to attempt honesty without insuring themselves against the consequences with sexual weapons. That is, a woman *may* be honest with a man she knows she attracts, but not with the woman who is impervious. I was so entirely sure of this that I said to myself once and for all, I don't want any women, ever, ever. I want to live. I want to be strong. And I want to indulge myself in my own particular vanity which is to despise evasions. If I manage to make myself physically presentable (it's only a bluff – I'm too used up with illness to be, really) men will indulge me in the whim of honesty. Stooping to the tricks of sex never seems so degrading as more subtle trickery. For one thing, it does no harm to confess them. It isn't necessary to lie to oneself.

Well, as I say, I had thoroughly made up my mind that it was impossible for *two* women to be honest in the same room – .

I'm not sentimental either, and I'm not insisting that we shall throw ourselves into each other's arms with cries of rapture which we don't feel. You're even a very different kind of person from me, and probably from your point of view, better. From my point of view of course, you aren't. But I do respect you. Just as I know myself to be worthy of respect, I feel very deeply that you are. I want to be your friend. Sometime when you are better, I want to talk to you about myself, and I shan't apologise for doing it.

We had so little time yesterday, and you felt so badly that I do not know whether or not enough was said about your visit to impress it on you that we want you so very, very much. It will do as much for us as I hope it will do for you. What I want is for you to try and arrange it so you can go back with us in about four or five weeks. It would be so much better for you to go directly with us when you aren't well, for we can look after you the little bit you'll need and have our voyage enlivened with a companion as well. You'll love Rio. You can't help it. When we were poorer I worked hard, but now we are a little better off we can be lazy like the natives, and you and I will have nothing to do but write. My mother lives with me, and she isn't a Bohemian like I am, but she is a very mousey retiring person, and my little boy is the dearest thing in the world.

I can't express what I think of Cyril, except that he will appreciate you more than ever you were appreciated. He does already. I don't care what man may have appreciated you, I never saw one with Cyril's real bigness and insight. So won't you help us begin to plan about your coming? Getting down there won't only do your insides good. It will do your work good.

Though the trip to Brazil did not materialize, Lola reciprocated Evelyn's feelings, and also became a staunch admirer of her work. Apart from her generous review of *Precipitations*, she joined the enthusiastic chorus which greeted the publication of *The Narrow House* in 1921.

Loudest in the chorus was Sinclair Lewis, who reviewed the novel ecstatically in the *New York Times Book Review*: 'Salute to Evelyn Scott! It would be an insult to speak with smug judiciousness of her "promise". She has done it! *The Narrow House* is an event, it is one of those recognitions of life by which life itself becomes the greater.'

Lewis' *Main Street* had been published a year earlier and had helped set a trend towards bleak examinations of small-town life, of which *The Narrow House* was perhaps the most extreme example. The reaction to the book from Main Street itself was predictably condemnatory. One Emma Alexander, a Kansas City librarian, wrote an incensed letter to the publishers saying that the book was degrading and was banned from their shelves: 'I have never seen worse in print [. . .] Man is prone to sin and it is the mission of our educators and leaders to uplift instead of degrade.' She concluded, 'Evelyn Scott no doubt described her own vile self.'

Probably the nightmarish relationships of the book owed much to Evelyn's childhood in Clarksville and New Orleans as neurosis and financial collapse enveloped her family. The child, May, is given the kind of life and subtlety of depiction by Evelyn which suggest a strong identification. She too is the victim of her mother's unwanted demands and attentions.

The relentless misery was too much for some readers. Theodore Dreiser described the novel as 'the grimmest and most acrid I have ever read', and a copy sent to D. H. Lawrence provoked a response which combined amusement and horror:

> Well, I think it's all vile, but true and therefore valuable [...] I feel it is white America's last word [...] I say this, The Narrow House made me hate the disease of love finally, for which, many thanks. Give me henceforth Mars and a free fight.... I didn't think your Women In Love review in The Dial very sensible. But there, we have different values. Why don't you just spit in the eye of the world and shit on the doorstep of the Narrow House [...] Even you are incomplete. A Narrow House without a water closet! [...] What a cockadoodling lot! Shut 'em all up in the W.C. and make 'em describe, in definite language, how they wipe their arses before you let 'em out. THE END OF THE NARROW HOUSE – Valissime!

After their brief correspondence, Lawrence borrowed the name of Cyril Scott, though nothing of the man, for his next novel, *Aaron's Rod*.

By this time Evelyn had quarrelled with *The Dial*; a split she explained on one occasion as a result of editorial disapproval of her article on Gilbert Cannan, on another as a result of Marianne Moore's disapproval of her morals. Whichever the case *The Narrow House* was hatcheted by their reviewer and they were unsympathetic toward her next two books. Evelyn's dislike of adverse criticism meant that *The Dial* joined her growing list of enemies.

She did not see the book as a deliberate excursion into a sordid world, but as an exercise in naturalism. In her portrayal of neurotic adults preying on a child she merely depicted commonplaces of her own childhood. She was deeply influenced by Freud and her view of the family concentrated on the sinister undercurrents which she felt were present when pretences were stripped away.

But she had a family of her own and a son who would also retain painful memories of a confused upbringing in Brazil and among the 'free souls' of the Village. He did not disguise his memories fictionally and, at the end of his life, composed a memoir of these years, grimmer and more acrid than his mother's first novel had been.

13
The Innate Awfulness of Everything

CREIGHTON SCOTT'S unpublished memoir, 'Confessions of an American Boy', paints a lurid, condemnatory child's eye view of Bohemian life. He prefaced it with a quotation from Isaiah: 'The fathers have eaten sour grapes, and the children's teeth are set on edge.' But he might well have quoted Burns: 'There's a cheild among you, taking notes, And, faith, he'll prent it.'

As remembered by Creighton the Scotts' Village apartment was the scene of frequent frenetic sexual activity, which would often spill over into his bedroom. On occasion he would have to give up his bed to impetuous couples and was once awoken by a pair of lovemakers at full tilt who were unaware that he was in the bed until he protested. From time to time he would be the subject of unwanted attentions from paedophiles of both sexes. At the age of six or seven he was the subject of an experiment to see whether he had grown beyond the pregenital stage of sexual development: he was placed naked on a bed with a girl of his own age, surrounded by a knot of curious adults. No sexual activity occurred, to the annoyance of the assembled group. Creighton detested most of his mother's friends, whom he recalls as overwhelmingly fleshly and interested to an obsessive degree in fornication.

Creighton blamed this libidinousness on the influence of misused Freudian ideas, which then dangled before the American intelligentsia the hallucination that repression might be abolished. The prevailing view of the child became not an innocent trailing clouds of glory but a mass of unformed sexual feelings awaiting development from one stage to another. Evelyn's conversation is reported as consisting almost exclusively of Freudian jargon, and behind much of the book is an attempt to refute Freud; ironically, since his mother would expend much energy in the thirties attempting to refute Marx. He felt that the cardinal principle of Freudian theory as interpreted by Evelyn and her friends was The Innate Awfulness of Everything, a phrase whose concoction he ascribes to his mother. Freudianism in their hands became a reductionist theory which transformed the mystery of sex into a set of predetermined responses, a belief system which they used for purposes of sadistic probing rather than as therapy. After the twenties these ideas were absorbed into society at large, leading to a cult of egoism which, Creighton felt, has blighted American life ever since.

The activities of the Villagers seem to have been standard Bohemian excesses, common to all times. But for Creighton, born in a wattle hut in Brazil and speaking Portuguese as his first language, the creaking bedsprings, embracing pairs and trios and the occasional attempt to introduce him into sexual activity resulted in an unbearable level of confusion. In later life he wished his upbringing had been normal, so at least he might have had something to rebel against. Instead he directed his rancour at the version of freedom offered by the Village crowd and at Freud, whose misapplied theories were responsible in his opinion for most of his youthful misery.

Evelyn does not seem to have been a progressive mother, for all her artistic and sexual progressiveness. Creighton recalled that a beating with a hairbrush could be expected when he annoyed her in some way. His dislike of his mother borders on hatred in the memoirs and the single bright spot on a morbid landscape is provided by his father. As *Life is too Short* indicates, Cyril had little sympathy for these goings-on and according to Creighton endured seven or nine triangular relationships only because he wanted to be with his son. The elopement had shut off his past with absolute finality and in a real sense there was nowhere else for him to go. There were frequent quarrels with Evelyn as he made no secret of his contempt for those around him; further-more, his low opinion of Freud placed him intellectually out of bounds to most of her friends.

The period of boarding out on a baby farm outside New York is also described with retrospective horror. He was dosed daily with opiated syrup and subjected to a rigorous regime of punishment and therapy. When he returned to the Brooklyn apartment which he shared with his father – Evelyn and Cyril were by this time living apart – he felt a hopeless craving come on about the time he would have received medication on the farm.

In his memoir, when he comes to assess the attitudes and achievements of those among whom he was raised, his venom becomes charged. In his opinion and experience the neo-Freudian stance was as anti-life as that of the neo-Puritans. He designated both as Urps, a term coined by his father which was a conflation of the word Urpuritanismus. Cyril had defined this as the primitive bedrock Puritan: 'a sub-species of man who knows what's good for you. And, by a marvellous coincidence, it always turns out to be what they prefer.' Creighton judged his mother as 'one hundred per cent pure Urp'.

The Village crowd were a self-conscious, self-appointed élite; millenarians who would often compare themselves to the early Christians. Their mission was the redefinition of America in their own image. Creighton observed: 'Such phrases are hackneyed now, but forty years ago America was being given so many New Dimensions and New Directions its shape was unimaginable and it must have been spinning like a gyroscope.'

And of the direction America took:

> It was a loathsome generation, whose outstanding trait will be remembered as their envy and distrust of their own posterity. All their doctrines, their theories and their endeavours were aimed at hampering and strait-jacketing succeeding generations, for in their infatuated self-complacency they could not conceive it possible that anyone might be worthy to succeed them [. . .]
>
> It was a giggling, impulsive movement against conformity, to which it was necessary to conform. And, mystical religious concepts apart, it was nearly indistinguishable from that of the Puritan America about which Sinclair Lewis wrote so well. And it was absolutely negative. The goal, the grail for which such persons strove, was merely to be non-Puritan [. . .]
>
> In circles where free love prevails, women are far less than chattels in my experience – they are more nearly a sort of

public convenience, like the subway or the Men's Room; and I have known a good many in my time who reached the point where they asked nothing else of life for the moment except to be allowed to menstruate in peace [. . .]

They are all harmless nature-lovers now, for their work is done. The world of today is far different from the one they inveighed against; knowledge is diffuse rather than diffused; morals and ethics are subjects the study of which is regarded with righteous contempt; nobody believes in anything but money, and even that declines in value day by day. It is harder to find an honest man than it was in the days of – – – – , and the fact is, the world has been quite thoroughly remade in the pattern they foresaw, and what they said about it then is true now. At last they are at peace with the Puritans, their former enemies, and as hope diminishes for the rest of us you can hear their paunches rumble euphetically with joy as they observe the example they set being followed more and more closely.

Lola Ridge and a few others were excluded from the condemnation, but included, and especially disliked, were Waldo Frank, Maxwell Bodenheim and Floyd Dell. It has been said that between 1920 and 1925, almost 50 per cent of the literature in America was written in Greenwich Village. Yet few of the Scott circle achieved anything permanent and their names survive as footnotes in other people's memoirs: work which had seemed to herald a new dawn sank in the bottomless pit of the Great Unread. Of the immediate group only Williams attained lasting stature and he was a weekend Bohemian rather on the periphery. Maxwell Bodenheim, especially detested by Cyril, survived as a Village landmark until the mid-fifties when, a bum and long-confirmed alcoholic, he died at the hands of a former mental patient who had become attached to his current lover. Most reverted to anonymity and normalcy and the more astute carved out careers in publishing or the press.

The jaundice of Creighton's memoir must be seen in the context of the later soured relationship between mother and son. Creighton saw nothing of his mother after 1949, and he did his best to avoid any contact with her. Most of the events in the memoir took place while Creighton was aged between six and thirteen and were recorded forty years later. A confused imagina-

tive child confronted with an alien adult world might well, in
hindsight, apply its own sinister construction to behaviour which
was merely boisterous or playful. A suspiciously large amount of
dialogue is totally recalled and there are one or two instances of
apparent false memory in operation. Ernest Hemingway is mentioned as being among the Village set, whereas all biographical
authorities place him in Chicago at this time. Nevertheless, the
condemnation of Village life is so sweeping and Creighton's
hatred of his mother and her circle so intense that the reader is
left in little doubt that a childhood among the 'free souls' proved
a painful and permanently scarring experience.

The Narrow House and Cyril's Cercadinho-written novel, *Blind
Mice*, were published in spring 1921 to critical rather than
commercial success. Cyril's job was uncongenial and under the
pressure of this and money problems he suffered a nervous
collapse. This had the effect of reuniting him with Evelyn.

The Scotts' friends were generally more affluent than they
and Evelyn began to borrow money to keep afloat – four
hundred and fifty dollars from Waldo Frank, one hundred and
fifty from Williams, two hundred from Swinburne Hale and
smaller sums from others. In this difficult situation it was Marie
T. Garland Hale, the wife of Swinburne Hale, a successful
lawyer who also wrote verse, who came to the rescue. She was a
millionairess in her own right, having married as her first
husband a major shareholder of the First National Bank of New
York, and an unconventional extrovert in character. Over the
next decade she would come to occupy a position in the lives of
the Scotts like that of Mabel Dodge Luhan in those of the
Lawrences.

She was impressed by what she knew of Cyril's varied background and asked him to become manager of her estate at
Buzzard's Bay. He gratefully accepted the offer and this venture
was to be as successful as his many other fresh starts in life. In
the year he spent there he reduced the annual deficit from
twenty thousand dollars to eight thousand. While at Buzzard's
Bay the Scotts received a small wage plus free accommodation
and produce and when they left they were granted a weekly
allowance of $25 which was instrumental in their survival over
the next decade. Oddly, Mrs Garland Hale did not like their

above 1 The Gracie Mansions,
Clarksville, Tennessee, birthplace
of Evelyn Scott; *right* 2 Cyril Kay-
Scott, *c.* 1920

3 Maude Thomas Dunn, Evelyn Scott's mother

4 Seely Dunn, her father

The changing faces of Evelyn
Scott: *above left* 5 Evelyn Scott,
c. 1920; *above right* 6 Evelyn
Scott, *c.* 1929; *right* 7 Evelyn
Scott, *c.* 1933 (*Eva Gay*)

left 8 Evelyn Scott, *c.* 1942

below 9 From a portrait in oils of Evelyn Scott, *c.* 1934 (*Breathe Upon These Slain*)

novels and neither, after a while, did she like Evelyn. But she became very fond of Cyril.

Life on the estate was chaotic and there was a constant stream of callers. Frequent exotic visitors included the Lebanese poet Kahlil Gibran, and Rose O'Neill, the outrageously theatrical inventor of the Kewpie Doll, an idea whose nationwide popularity had earned her a fortune. There were nearly a hundred buildings on the estate and so many cars that a free private filling station had been built. Dress and mealtimes were informal in the extreme. Evelyn reported to Lola shortly after arrival: 'We spent the first three days at Mrs Garland's large and very beautiful country house surrounded by automobiles and Arcadian millionaire children who go barefoot and wash their own dishes. Mrs Garland has two picturesque silent sons and one young viking daughter – altogether the most characterful examples of the idle rich I ever saw.'

One of the silent sons was Charles Garland, an intense and idealistic youth who, when he reached his majority, gave away his paternal inheritance of one million dollars to set up a fund to promote radicalism in America. Consequently penniless, he started subsistence farming to keep his wife and child, but his marriage and the farm collapsed with the appearance of another woman on the scene. Evelyn thinly fictionalised the downfall of this Utopian experiment in her third novel, *The Golden Door*, an act which did little to endear her to Barley (as he was known) or to his parents. It was an ironic revenge of fate that the Garland fund was to be responsible for financing *New Masses*, the most effective vehicle of thirties literary communism, a movement whose influence Evelyn spent much energy attacking.

But snakes lurked in the grass even in this eccentric and moneyed Arcadia. The outgoing Marie Garland and the introverted Swinburne Hale were proving incompatible and eventually a crisis occurred. Swinburne Hale left for Bermuda where he bought a large decaying mansion which he invited Cyril to help rehabilitate. After some indecision the Scotts took up the offer and their lengthy expatriation began.

Buzzard's Bay was within easy reach of Greenwich Village which they frequently revisited. Their time as Villagers was relatively brief yet, in spite of continuous trauma, artistically fruitful. Evelyn had made many friends and also a number of highly placed enemies. She had established herself as a writer with a future; one toward whom the arbiters of advanced taste, Sinclair Lewis, Dreiser and Mencken, looked favourably. A form of relationship with Cyril had survived everything and, against the odds, both had continued to write prolifically. At Buzzard's Bay Cyril had vented his dislike of Bohemia in a satire called *Sinbad* and Evelyn had completed a draft of *Narcissus*, a sequel to *The Narrow House*. Expatriation was a matter of chance rather than choice but, unconsciously, they were treading a path which many American writers would follow in the coming decade.

14

Bermuda Triangle

~~~~~~

IN 1922 THE island of Bermuda had about 20,000 inhabitants. 12,000 of these were the Negro descendants of slaves brought there by the British; of the remainder, several thousand were fishermen of Portuguese descent. The main town was Hamilton, which served as a base for the British Navy. The British were, and still are, administrators and social arbiters, tasks which they carried out as they still do in pale imitation of standards which had become outmoded in the mother country many years before. Evelyn, the radical, was appalled: 'There is no system of free education, no divorce, no anything later than eighteen twenty. The English here are the Governor, a number of bonehead military officials and the people who run the naval yard. They are scandalised at mixed bathing, at women who smoke, etc.' Even then the island had a flourishing tourist trade though this barely affected the remote part where the Scotts lived.

Ely Mansions was a dilapidated estate in Somerset Parish. They occupied this rent-free and, in addition, received a small allowance. In return they were expected to renovate the house and put its grounds in order. They were also given a plot of land on which to build and Cyril constructed a large cottage out of local stone which they eventually occupied. Evelyn recorded that sanitation and water supplies were extremely primitive.

Their remoteness and the sharp, brilliant colours of the landscape constantly reminded Evelyn of Brazil and she was soon to make good use of these recollections. For the present, in an atmosphere she found ideal for sustained writing, she completed

Narcissus and began the third part of her trilogy, *The Golden Door*. But, as usual, emotional complication was in the air. Their benefactors, Swinburne Hale and Marie Garland, were playing out the last act of their marital drama at full volume in the background and even in this barely populated region it was not long before Evelyn discovered a new lover.

The first few months were peaceful. Though sinking into debt, Evelyn was working solidly and planning the next move. To Lola she suggested, 'What if we all struggle along a while and finally all migrate to Europe together? Lewis Gannett is back and reports everything in New York having gone to Paris. e e cummings, Dos Passos, Harold Stearns, Edna Millay, Cuthbert Wright and several dozen more – all apparently impecunious and all do it. We ought to find the secret.'

She was also worried about her unpopularity in the New York book world: 'I tell you, Lola, I am more friendless than I was the day I hit New York in a literary sense, for I apparently do nothing but pile up enemies in places of power.' She had quarrelled with Horace Liveright, publisher of *The Narrow House,* and *Narcissus* was brought out by Harcourt, Brace & Co. in 1922. *The Golden Door* was finally published in 1925 by Thomas Seltzer, since Alfred Harcourt refused it on the grounds of its limited appeal and because it might be a candidate for legal suppression.

There was a flow of visitors from New York and Lola kept Evelyn up to date with events there. She had become joint editor of *Broom*, a radical literary review, though Evelyn had unfortunately offended her fellow editors too deeply for her to contribute. But Lola wrote glowingly of a young girl assistant on the magazine, barely out of her teens, in whom she detected a great deal of promise. Her name was Kay Boyle.

Traffic between New York and Bermuda was not only one way, and Evelyn sent a new friend in need over to Lola with the following innocuous introduction:

Say, dearest, I almost forgot, another lost soul we are sending to you. A little man called Owen Merton, about thirty I should judge, a Scotch Welshman from New Zealand who had been for the last year living in Flushing where his wife recently died and left him with two children. He is very hard up, very naive and genuine, as obscene as Bill Williams, and in all respects an interesting child with real if not stupendous talent. He had been working fiendishly hard at watercolour and some of his things are very successful. He is as poor as the rest of us and has been trying to eke it out with landscape gardening. It would mean tremendous things to him to be reproduced in *Broom* as he had been snubbed by some of the people – Daniels Gallery, etc. He is bugs on Cézanne and says very illuminating things about him. Admires Charlie Demuth very much. Not all of Merton's things would reproduce among modern stuff but a few would. We want him to show them to you.

Owen Merton's two children were called Tom and John Paul. John Paul was too young to travel and had been left in America with his grandparents but Tom, aged seven, had accompanied his father and lived with him in a boarding house on the other side of the island from the Scotts. Though Owen Merton's art is now forgotten, he survives in a vivid portrait in an autobiography which his son wrote many years later. Like Creighton, Tom was to rebel against a confused upbringing, but in his case the revolt was taken to a more extreme conclusion. After education and a period on the Bohemian fringe, he embraced Catholicism, became a priest and finally accepted the harsh vows of Trappist monasticism. As Thomas Merton, he was to be the most influential figure of his time in American literary Catholicism and would chart his spiritual evolution in a remarkable autobiography, *The Seven Storey Mountain*.

In this, with his mother a fading infant memory and his solid, unimaginative grandparents described with faint contempt, Thomas Merton depicts his father as the lodestar of his life. He is portrayed as a near saint, a Catholic manqué whose presence was felt during Thomas Merton's first major religious experience, which occurred in a Rome hotel room a year after his father's death. *The Seven Storey Mountain* hints that the extremity of Merton's religious commitment was partly due to the ordeals of his early life but, like many autobiographers, he proved circumspect in dealing with them.

He was born at Prades, in the South of France, in 1915. This was an inauspicious year of birth in a country where armies were enmeshed in mud only several hundred miles away and it was a poor time to earn a living as an artist, as Owen was trying to do.

Owen Merton had left his native New Zealand for London and had then gone to Paris to study art with P. Tudor-Hart between 1911 and 1914. Here he had met and married an American fellow student, Ruth Jenkins. He had achieved some success in the English art world but financial independence remained a distant prospect. Prades was an experiment in rural self-sufficiency which failed badly and the young couple and their child came close to starvation before they were baled out by the Jenkins family and were able to go to America in 1916.

They lodged with the Jenkins household in America, but relations between the impractical Owen and his in-laws were strained by his continued dependence on them. Eventually the couple moved into a house, little more than a shack, in Flushing, Long Island, and Owen tried to support the family by landscape gardening, work as a church organist and as pianist in a movie theatre. A second child was born, but the marriage was beginning to show the strain of unrelenting poverty. When Ruth Jenkins died in 1921, Owen was racked by guilt that his inability to support his family might have been a contributory cause and by the knowledge that the marriage had grown very threadbare. Thomas Merton barely remembered his mother and the autobiography suggests little sense of loss. She seems to have been cold and intellectual, unlike the highly emotional Owen.

Her death freed Owen in part from family responsibilities which he was temperamentally and financially unable to sustain. John Paul stayed behind and Owen and Tom set off for Bermuda, where Owen planned to paint full-time.

After meeting Evelyn, Owen began to spend increasing amounts of time with the Scotts and eventually moved into their house. At some stage, he became Evelyn's lover. Cyril appears to have been amicable about this, since at this time, doubtless with Merton's encouragement, he began a new career as a watercolourist. Tom Merton stayed alone at the boarding house for some time, then his father brought him to live at Ely Mansions with the woman who was to be, effectively, his stepmother. Tom did not like her though a strong friendship grew between him and Creighton. Both were seven and their respective wandering lives had given neither a chance to form ordinary boyhood contacts. Creighton recalled:

We built a sea-garden, had a very leaky boat in secret, stole a hundredweight of copper rivets from a boatbuilder and buried them as treasure (money is made of copper) – map and everything. It was Tom who planted in me the seed of un-Americanism. His [Owen's] in-laws had been heartless about his mother's death, and as they were Americans he hated everything they stood for. He and I used to draw elaborate pictures of naval battles between HMS something and USSS something. The extra S made USSS stand for United States Shit Ship, and the American navy always went down with all hands, due to scandalous seamanship and wholesale cowardice.

From the outset, Tom refused to accept Evelyn's assumption of a maternal role. Tom and Creighton shared the same bed and Creighton remembered that Tom would often keep him awake, gritting his teeth in fury at Evelyn's dictates. Creighton felt that his mother's treatment of Tom was one of the most unpleasant of her activities and drew a horrifying picture of Evelyn *in loco parentis*:

The fact is that Tom's own mother, apart from being dead, was an unsubstantial phantasm in her eyes, that had never existed or should have existed. I can remember his being punished for crying – it may have been over his bereavement for all that any of the rest of us knew – for losing his appetite, for being late to his meals, and an infinite number of things that other children are reprimanded for but no more. What must have made it insufferable to him is that when I did the same things, I got off scot-free, and the fact is that in dealing with him, my mother was ruthlessly and uncouthly indifferent to whatever his private sorrows and obsessions may have been; a fact I have remembered all my life. The truth seems to have been that these sorrows offended her because she was excluded from them and he would not talk to her about them; and to the diseased ego of the Freudian puritan, as well as that of the Calvinist one, there is nothing quite so unforgiveable and deserving of the more refined agonies of the mind than not spilling out your viscera on the table, conveniently near the reading lamp, for detailed inspection. Whether Tom realised it or not, he was in my

opinion subjected to a knowing and adept brutality, calibrated
to his youth, his ignorance, and the obscure grief and
uncertainty that evidently consumed him, and even my father
expostulated and said he had had enough of vivisection in his
scientific days. Tom was outside the vacuum, and I was in it,
and therefore he was in peril while I was safe.

Quite apart from the actual deeds, there is something
bestial, I think, in usurping the position of a dead mother by
force majeure, over the anguished protests of the child, and
punishing him for not liking it. She used to have tantrums
behind his back, too, and I remember her screaming at
Merton. 'I'm sick of his damned mother. Sick of her, sick of
her, sick of her! I hate her, hate her, hate her, do you hear?'
That was what mattered, not what Tom felt. This was a woman
who sneered at jealousy and despised it as infantile.

Perhaps this short episode led to the bloodless suicide and
the Seven Storey Mountain – I would not know, for I never saw
Tom again. Evidently he gained a new life, as one is said to do
after one dies, for which I am thankful. In my late twenties,
when she and I were still on speaking terms, her reminiscences
about Tom's 'badness' and intractability were all accompanied
by little unctuous giggles, like that of a schoolgirl using a dirty
word for the first time.

Evelyn found Tom and Creighton to be difficult children, but
no witness remains to give evidence whether she was a cruel
mother or simply a highly strung woman faced with two trouble-
some seven-year-olds. Though Creighton's account is harrow-
ing, it is the judgement of a child on a parent, set down many years
after the events described. The whole period, nearly a year, was
omitted from *The Seven Storey Mountain* and was unrecorded in
any of Thomas Merton's published or unpublished writing. Cyril
and Evelyn are briefly alluded to as friends of Owen who were
'literary people and artists', but the nature of his father's involvement with them is ignored. A description of the triangle would
not have enhanced the idealised portrait of Owen which he drew
and his views of Evelyn might have involved a large lapse from
Christian charity. As so often, the truth about her proved too
complicated for inclusion and, like Waldo Frank and Williams,
Merton suppressed her in his memoir.

Some of Owen Merton's letters have survived and Evelyn fictionalised him twice. She described her intentions in a letter to Lola: '[...] I am going to write a book about Merton who has given me such wonderful data about himself that my imagination is quite gripped by it. He has such very immediate reactions to things and is so graphic in his recollections. He thinks in three dimensions, concretely, and always with the eyes. I think it will be a fascinating occupation to make a portrait. Not a novel of intent, which I have hitherto been inclined to – but an individual portrait such as a painter might make.'

She carried this out in a never-published book, *The Grey Riddle*, whose artist-hero, Pete Johnson, is based on Merton. Since Owen was present during its composition as an active collaborator, the book is presumably more accurate than most *romans-à-clef*. Pete Johnson is a man torn by conflicting desires; a committed artist barely able to function in the world. There are hints of a bisexual past, and indications that his marriage was opposed by parents and relatives on both sides. A more fanciful portrait is drawn in *Eva Gay* where Merton is depicted as an archetypal half-crazed genius, the rather ludicrously named Evan Garrett, 'a fumbling, brutal and fragmentary man'.

In Merton's dedication to his art there is some affinity with the austere portrait drawn by his son, but what is missing in Thomas Merton's account is the disorder, indecision and poverty reflected in both fictional studies and in Owen Merton's own correspondence. Owen himself would eventually have to make a decision of conscience but the choice was not to be forced upon him for some years.

The adult trio did not allow domestic complexity to impede industry. Evelyn completed *The Golden Door* and began work on *Escapade*. She also wrote fifteen short stories, which were not particularly successful. Money was short as usual and the absorption into the household of the penniless Owen Merton did not help. However, early in 1923 Merton returned to New York and arranged a show of his Bermuda watercolours at the Daniel Gallery. The preface to the exhibition catalogue was written by Cyril, indicating at least some warmth toward the man who had supplanted him. The Daniel Gallery was prestigious and the paintings sold well. Almost simultaneously Evelyn received an advance on *Escapade* from Thomas Seltzer and, suddenly free from penury, the trio turned their thoughts toward Europe again. For the first time, a move there was possible with the aid of Marie Garland's allowance. Tom was sent back to his grandparents, and Cyril squared the triangle by bringing along Ellen Kennan, a New York girlfriend. In June 1923 the party set off for a visit to Europe which was to be lengthier than any of them envisaged.

15

Great Expatriations

THE GROUP crossed the Atlantic on a steamer which travelled
via Africa, Gibraltar and Naples, where the party sought confir-
mation of Innate Awfulness by taking a carriage ride around the
worst slums. Merton had bad memories of Naples. On a previous
visit he had contracted sunstroke and had frequently been
robbed. But Ellen Kennan spoke Italian and liked the Italians and
the two began to disagree. Evelyn was duly appalled by the city:

> Such streets, Lola. Palermo had the same narrowness, the
> same tortuousness, but its filth was new and bright and
> subdued. Old Naples was a decayed body – sharp and strong
> with people living in it as in maggotty meat – people that ran in
> and out of dark windowless holes that were meat stalls and
> butcher's shops. In every shop a shrine like a kind of ikon with
> an electric bulb glaring stolidly in front of it. Such meat shops
> – harsh pieces of red flesh, dingy tiles, crusts of flies, and
> always, always visible in the shallow depths as we stared in from
> the carriage, the worn picture of the saint on the wall above the
> counter at the back. Such cadaverous women, such anemic
> children, such an absence of any joy in light or life – nothing
> anywhere but a rich and crowded hideousness. There were
> shrines on the outsides of houses too, shrines that were dingy
> and fly specked, and beneath them also burned an electric
> light. The vegetables exposed were soiled and old and there
> was charcoal dust. Some of the streets, like the ones I remem-
> ber in Lisbon, climbed endless stairs with the banners of

laundered clothes rising tier on tier until they waved at last in the merciless light. Palermo reminded me of Rio de Janeiro on a smaller scale. It was young. Naples was used as I never saw a city used before. There was not a fresh face, not a fresh house front – nothing that had not come to the end of itself and sprouted again, like a tree that is half-felled but struggles yet to a little harsh growth. The stinks I had anticipated, I didn't find, in actuality. It was a visual aroma that I mostly got – black olives, wine jugs, basket makers, chair weavers, cobblers, smithies, wood sellers, all crowded in one street – court yards that had the faint illumination of decay – and people, people in rooms the depth of a wall, people who were crowded helplessly into the street, while those in Palermo willingly lived in it.

Awfulness notwithstanding, Evelyn was glad to be away from the 'destructive agitation' of New York. When the boat reached the South of France, the group made its way to Collioure, a town in the Pyrenees which Merton knew well. It was an art colony, of the kind which flourished in that region in the interwar years, and was filled with penniless painters, mostly of indifferent talent. Here Evelyn experienced her own peculiar brand of homesickness and felt, for the first time, the dawning of an American identity. To Lola she wrote:

For some funny reason, I never thought about America as America, a unit, a country with people in it, not people in a country, as I have since we came here. I suppose I had no sense of America when I left New Orleans, and this is the first time I have felt absolutely removed from it, since I left New York, for Bermuda was too close. It is voluptuous like an old lady's memories. I used to feel that way about Brazil, but didn't know it would come so quickly about this. I don't think I ever knew there was a racial America before. Lower Broadway with a lost gull I once saw flying over it has become as symbolic as the mountains we saw along the African coast. I suppose this is the first time I ever indulged romanticism about my native land. Anyway, the more I see of other countries, or this one other country, the more magnificently awful my own country appears to be.

This was a strange form of romanticism. Ellen Kennan decided that she had heard enough incessant art-talk at Collioure and left for Berlin to visit her old friend, Emma Goldman. She had especial problems with Merton, whose devotion to painting bordered on monomania. Evelyn continued to work in collusion with Merton on *The Grey Riddle*, but France proved to be neither as cheap nor as warm as had been hoped. So, as winter approached, the group crossed the Mediterranean to Algeria and travelled south until they came to rest in a small rented house in the oasis settlement of Bou Saada.

The appearance of an unveiled American woman and child accompanied by two men must have been a shock to the intensely conservative Muslim villagers. Household complexities considerably heightened when Waldo Frank came over from Spain on an extended visit. With common-law husband, present lover and past lover under one roof on the edge of the Sahara, a ménage was created which rivalled in oddity that of Cercadinho.

Creighton was sent to the local Arab-French school where, not unnaturally, he was something of an outsider. He was unprepared for the level of violence in the blackboard jungle of Bou Saada. A schoolmate was beaten to death by an Arab teacher and Creighton once opened the door of the house to find a youth's corpse outside with neck slit ear to ear lying in a pool of blood. He found an ally in the son of their cook who, being a Jew, was similarly ostracised. Religious bigotry in the town was so intense that Jews and Muslims segregated even their rubbish tips. Creighton began carrying a knife for protection and, after a stoning incident, ran away for several days. When he was found, the disappearance was explained as his having been 'lost' and it formed the basis for a children's book on which Cyril and Evelyn collaborated, *In the Endless Sands*. Creighton later recalled Bou Saada as 'a God-forsaken place'.

Though he was unhappy there, for the adults it was a perfect place to work. They had unfortunately forgotten that the desert climate is not necessarily warm in winter, especially at night. Waldo wrote that he nearly froze to death and a snowstorm was greeted by a burst of hysterics from Evelyn. But there were few distractions and the landscape and local society were so alien that it was several months before Evelyn could record her impressions in a letter to Lola. Thomas Merton felt that his father's best work was done in Algeria, from where he sent exotic gifts home to his sons. He also sent home payments to the Jenkinses, and tried to keep up two insurance policies which he had taken out on his life.

Evelyn's letters from Bou Saada contain a good deal of retrospection. The presence of Waldo Frank stimulated some thoughts on their affair which, as far as she was concerned, was over: 'My mind went back to last year when Waldo, after trying to revive lovemaking, said "Won't you promise to write something on me, a brochure or something. To feel your mind at work on my books is like an exquisite sexual sensation." It was too much. He can't get it into his head that I am done with him as far as exquisite sexual sensations go.'

Frank had evidently taken his usual course and mythicised their relationship: 'His mix-up with me is a world event of a "Greek" (me, ye gods) meeting a great Hebrew prophet, a pagan encountering a Jew.' She caricatured Frank for a second time in *Herbert Young*, a sketch in a volume of novellas called *Ideals*. Though concerned almost entirely with New York life, the book was written at Bou Saada as the fact of exile turned Evelyn's imagination back to memories of America.

The Arab world of North Africa was responsible for a fine travel essay, 'To Kenitra', later published in the *Yale Review*. The evils of colonialism and the contempt of the *colons* for the Arabs were dwelled upon, though privately Evelyn was repelled by the casual brutality of Arab life and the low status accorded to women. She briefly adopted a boy and girl called Ali and Fatma, but the boy would not take orders from a woman so her commands had to be relayed via Creighton. Both children proved unassimilable and were later passed on to more suitable foster parents.

Evelyn was impervious to the call of Islam, which has seduced so many travellers. She wrote to Lola that 'Mohammedanism is horrible to a Western mind. Poverty accepted, slavery of women accepted, disease accepted, and death just the tossing of unconfined bodies into the scratched earth where rain and the dogs go later to dig it up.' In an unpublished essay, 'New England in Algeria', she compared the Arab mentality to that of the Puritans and found both wanting: 'When man is Puritan, he becomes, in ways Freudianly explicable, a sadist.' Of the Muslim male she wrote, 'His utter contempt for woman is, in her intimate functional relation to him, a species of self-contempt.' Over-all she concluded that the Arab was merely an indifferent New England Puritan, held in restraint by his contempt for any progress that was not inspired by religion.

When spring came the group travelled by train back to Algiers and returned to Banyuls, a Pyreneean town ten miles from Collioure. At last Merton had aroused interest in the London commercial art world and, taking the last of his money, went to England to organise an exhibition. Bou Saada had been most difficult for him. His money problems had been alleviated when the Garland Fund sent a grant, but then he had mysteriously fallen ill and come close to death; possibly the first onset of the brain tumour eventually to claim his life. Two sets of paintings mailed from Algeria were lost in the mail and there was no alternative to a visit in person. He saw Roger Fry and interested him in both his own and Cyril's work, sold several paintings and arranged a show which was to take place at the Leicester Galleries in the following year. Cyril went to Paris for medical treatment, then joined Merton in London where he too met Roger Fry. The two men impressed each other and Cyril was to write the catalogue introduction for Fry's first exhibition some years later.

While in Paris, Cyril had arranged a show of his own at the Galeries Vildrac. When he left London he returned to Paris and rented a studio which was to be his base for the next few years. Evelyn visited Paris several times but never took the city to heart. Creighton spent the next years shuttled between his father and his mother, a child adjunct to a world of self-obsessed artists whom he damned in his memoir:

In those days my parents and their friends, with exceptions I shall write about later, were not interested in any motives but their own. There was a sort of cruel innocence about them such as a shark or a crocodile may be said to have, or any animal too low on the evolutionary scale to be held accountable for what it does to other creatures. Compassion was not merely at a discount, it was repudiated as vaguely evil: a perversion cunningly foisted upon mankind by the dark conspiracies of Christianity and Judaism. The value of any ethical system, like that of Christians and Jews, was judged by the extent men strayed from it [. . .]

There was a candour about their absorption in themselves
that fell just short of being endearing; and as they did not
understand too well the available panaceas, they did not do
very much except sit around on studio couches dreaming of
wonderful things to do, like Kipling's bandar-log. Action was
less to their taste than talking of their disease, which was disillusionment – a poignant weltschmerz – and if their wounds
could theoretically be healed. Like any other hypochondriacs
they liked their symptoms too much to seek cures.

As the talk of materialists so often does, theirs possessed
an overpoweringly imprecise quality, of pregnant opacity, at
once gluey and racy, like freshets of sludge. Evenings in the
shabby studios of my boyhood were filled with a mumble of
querulous self-diagnosis, such as one hears on the sun-porch
of a convalescent home; interspersed with erotic sniggers
whenever someone managed to work a little apposite smut
into context, or Harlequin got in a tweak at Columbine

Few of his parents' circle escape censure in a memoir seeth-
ing with bitterness against 'the adult delinquents of my youth'.
With the innate conservatism of childhood he most fondly
remembered the ordinary citizens who found themselves on the
periphery of the group. There was Stephania, his Brazilian
nurse, and Mr Weizenboden, the janitor of their New York
apartment who saved him from molestation at the hands of a
questing paedophile, one of Evelyn's friends. In Collioure he
was drawn to Father Duchamp, the hapless priest of the town's
remarkable church. Its belfry was graced with a cupola whose
over-all effect was so phallic that Father Duchamp periodically
tried to raise money to have it replaced. The Freudian significance of this did not escape Salvador Dali, who painted it, nor
Waldo Frank, who frequently visited from Spain.

In Paris Creighton became friendly with an old German
infantry sergeant who, having lost one arm, painted with the
other. He gave Creighton a set of tin soldiers which the boy
cherished but which were broken up as 'unsuitable toys' by one
of his father's girlfriends. He had exchanged some with a
neighbouring boy for a 'progressive' educational toy, which he
destroyed with a hammer, having quickly exhausted its
potentialities. Progressive pedagogy was more gestured at than

10 Cyril Kay-Scott/
Frederick Creighton
Wellman, *c.* 1942

11 Waldo Frank

above left 12 William Carlos Williams, *c.* 1923;
above right 13 Owen Merton,
left 14 Thomas Merton

above 15 Emma Goldman,
c. 1932; *right* 16 Alexander
Berkman, *c.* 1932

17 Squadron Leader John Metcalfe, *c.* 1943

18 Jean Rhys in Dominica, 1936

practised in the Scott household, but Creighton would have none of it.

Most of this time he spent with Cyril, for whom he had a genuine, if not uncritical, fondness. In Creighton's opinion his father's main weakness was that he was attracted to the wrong women. The 'stepmother' most warmly remembered by Cyril and Creighton was a Swiss woman called Elsa, who came from a well-to-do Catholic family. She became involved with Cyril shortly after he set up his Paris studio, and accompanied him on many of his European and North African painting expeditions. Her Catholicism prevented their marriage and she died in the late twenties, while Cyril was on a temporary visit to America. He never returned to Europe afterwards.

Evelyn and Owen Merton moved once more to Collioure, and then on to Béziers. Presumably this last move was for reasons of economy, since Béziers was a dull industrial town with little to commend itself to the artist. It was on one of her forays from here that she first met Kay Boyle, of whom she had heard in Lola's letters. Kay Boyle had married a Frenchman and was living outside Paris, a very junior member of the expatriate set. The two women arranged to meet, and Kay Boyle's memoir, in *Being Geniuses Together*, records their encounter in the only published pen-portrait of Evelyn in these years. It is a remarkable portrait which, in a few paragraphs, encompasses the many facets and contradictions of Evelyn's character:

Lola wrote to me that Evelyn was living in the South of France, or perhaps it was Spain at that moment, and she sent me her address. And so a correspondence began between us and a rather hostile if dedicated friendship that lasted with some lapses, for the next forty years. It ended the week of Evelyn's death. I had shown my first novel to no one and now I gave it the title of *The Imponderables*, and I sent it to Evelyn to read. The brilliance and the ruthlessness of her criticism so excited me that I began the book again at the beginning, and I wrote it entirely over. She had said that a veil hung between my work and the reader, and that I would have to tear that veil away before my writing could have any value. Night and day, week in, week out, I worked at the tearing away of that veil, not only in the hopelessly laboured

Imponderables (as I remember it) but in the new books and the poetry as well.

Once, when Evelyn was passing through Paris, she – who had so little herself – sent me the money to join her and her entourage for a few days there. But it was not an easy visit. One was aware at every instant of the nervous complexities of Evelyn's marital, and sexual, and professional lives, and in the smoke-filled, crowded hotel room I found it impossible even to hear what was being said. Perhaps I had lived too long in an almost unbroken inner silence, and now in my own confusion and insecurity I trembled for Evelyn's shattered depths. Was she wife, lover, mother, or none of these things, or all of them? It was difficult for me to determine, although all the elements and all the protagonists were there. Each meal we had, in modest restaurants, was taken over by her young son's loud and steady hiccoughing. Evelyn would accuse him of doing this in order to disrupt all conversation, and perhaps it was true, but it seemed to me quite a normal retaliation for having been given the name of Jigeroo.

The reality of our friendship resided in our letters, and this may have been because each of us was writing not to a stranger but to another facet of herself. In Paris we were abruptly two separate human beings, women with actual faces, voices, and we must look into each other's eyes and decide whether or not we believed in what we actually found there, whether we were comforted or discomforted. Evelyn in the flesh before me (was she ten or fifteen years older than I, or more, or less?) had neither the delicacy of bone nor the subtlety of wit of Marianne Moore. She had neither the saintlike head nor the burning presence of Lola Ridge, nor Lola's shining aura of belief. She seemed to me desperately intellectual, as these women I loved were not, and I decided this was because of her more formal education. She had been a college student at the time she eloped with a married professor, Cyril Scott. This I had learned from *Escapade*. But now, in which direction could she possibly go, I asked myself, in the intellectual uproar of her life? She had exchanged her dreams, her unseen world, for something I could not name. The first day she told me that she had seen McAlmon the night before, and that she had known him in New York before his marriage, but that he was always alien and cold. Remote, like a homosexual, she said. No, I said; that I don't believe. She said she didn't believe it either, but she could find no explanation of why no fire was ever struck between them, as it had been between her and Bill Williams, for instance. She wanted McAlmon to respond, she said; she wanted him to be seduced in the mind at least. She was asking surrender of him, as she asked it insidiously, with a terrible, terrible hunger, of everyone she met. But I was asking a great deal of women too that year. I didn't want them to use 'little' adjectives, such as Katherine Mansfield used, so that the universe itself was diminished; and I didn't want women sashaying around to the right and the left, with an eye for what flicker of response the flesh of all and sundry gentlemen might give.

One of Evelyn's party was Louise Theis, a New York friend from her days in the Village. Louise and her Austrian-born husband Otto had moved to London where they worked on an English weekly magazine, *The Outlook*. Largely because of their influence, *The Outlook*, by no means a modernist journal, came to publish the work of many Paris-based American expatriates and the Theis apartment in Temple Bar became an English outpost of the Paris–NewYork axis. A year after the meeting with Kay Boyle, Evelyn was visiting the Temple Bar apartment when her 'bête noire' McAlmon came by. He recalled the encounter acidly in his part of *Being Geniuses Together*: 'Miss Scott, vibrant-voiced and intense, would be significant about a book she was writing. *The Wave*, which I read in part in manuscript, I found to be probably the world's dullest book with its horrible "spiritual" messages beneath its hack pretences. Possibly she believed it created history, but her intensities and significances always made me squirmy. She'd be more restful if she'd just admit her mediocrity.'
Evelyn was not alone in being subjected to scathing judgement in the memoir. James Joyce, whose amanuensis and drinking partner McAlmon had been, dismissed the book as 'the office boy's revenge'. Yet while McAlmon's other work has slid into oblivion, the memoir remains still read; an eye-witness testimony of the mythic nexus described in its title, the geniuses of the 'lost generation'.

The expatriate wave in Paris seemed to reach a crest in 1924 and 1925, just after the reverberations of the complete publication of *Ulysses* had spread through the Anglophone intelligentsia. It is surprising that Evelyn did not spend more time in Paris given that so many old Village friends were there. Personal enmities may account for this for, through *Contact Editions*, McAlmon had become quite a power in the community. The expatriates contained a large contingent who were full-time drinkers and part-time artists and endless afternoons and nights of tipsy café argument would have been anathema to her dedication to Art. But the visit to Paris, and the meeting with Kay Boyle, turned Evelyn's thoughts homeward once more and in a letter to Lola she surveyed the latest cultural manifestations with her usual acerbic eye:

Lola, darling, you ought to see what a hungry light in the eyes inquires for the postman and sees if it is really the postscript you promised me. I feel awfully warm and comfortable with another letter from you and kind of, now that your address is so familiar, as if you couldn't get away from me again. I feel as if talking to East 7th, I'm talking closer up.

[. . .] Well, I haven't had any report on The Grey Riddle yet, and if you don't get it though, I will thank God for everything with all my heart for YOUR reading, and Davy's if he likes. If you ever let prophetic Waldo smell anything of mine, I'll come as near being mad at you as I can ever be knowing you. You must understand, Lola, that I'm doing my best to leave alone and be left alone, and I am not having Waldo playing his little heavenly mud pies and getting hisself all muddied up and seraphic with any more of my business. He is a very little boy and a very sensitive intelligent one, but he is a very, very naughty and malicious little boy because he would have been a very good little boy if his vanity hadn't obliged him to appear perfect in his own eyes and also to have a radiocommunication with God Almighty, his own private line. So while I think he is a very fine writer at his best, I think he is a very punk person, just five inches high, and his methods of attack made you feel you had fleas in your clothes and no way to defend yourself, you not being an angel baby god and all, but very vulnerable.

Well, I think the same, only different, of Bill Williams, and he would be the last person any of us would see in Paris. That day I met him at your house, I suddenly realised, sentimentality despite, that he was just exactly what he always was and always would be. Therefore any attempt to communicate with him would end like every other attempt, would end in getting that perfectly inane response of quick emotion which he doesn't understand himself, which makes him look like a wired jumping-jack with broken strings and arms and legs going feebly in all directions at once. Then he would recover and say that Marianne's work is good because he can't understand it, or that Bob McAlmon is the best artist he knows, or that women can't write anyway, or that – finally – he himself is a fool and knows it, or that he expects to be considered a great man when he dies and have a monument in Rutherford or a plate on his house. So –

I wouldn't go nearer that bunch than the plague. Last Spring, Sug [Evelyn's pet name for Cyril] saw Sylvia Beach and she evinced curiosity to behold my countenance, but that is the *Little Review* worshipping stuttering and homosexuality, and the English crowd with a cult of caddishness, like Aldous Huxley, while not forgetting any of the time to remind you it is a gentleman by birth at least and has all the advantages of Oxford erudition.

I wonder when, if ever, people will feel that art is not only TRUTH in a Kantian category, but that truth just is, alive in your isness, and that it isn't a cult, nor a vulgarity, a moral or a nonmoral, but just the articulation of the full and continuous actuality of the human being, sensation simultaneous with thought and the subtler emotions that analysis reveals but can't present. I'm sick of CULTS.

Kay Boyle lent me Bill Williams' *Great American Novel.* I thought it began magnificently, sort of sweeping down a precipice to destruction, a Ford car like a juggernaut, and all the lights of Jersey and Manhattan making crazy circles upward, standing even overhead as the car rushed past them with a suicidal radiance. Then, suddenly, juggernaut stands still, has a puncture in the tire or something curfluey with the engine. It won't dash to destruction at all. The great circles of flying buildings, windows, skylines, grain elevators and railway tracks stand still also. Excitement very weak now. Oh, yes, where was I? Shouting oyia. Oh, yes, and I'll tell you something about the absurdity of advertising. Oh, yes. Stutterings. Marianne Moore, Miss Moore, I mean Marianne. And Alfred Kreymborg. He's owed me money for a long time and I've never resented him enough to collect it so I must love him. He's a great poet.

Suddenly Mr Buffalo Bill Williams, the great tamer of the vanities of America, has just become nothing at all, a kind of flatulent effigy of his own patent medicine. Well, I did have an idea about these things, but damn it all, Walt Whitman was not consistent so why should I be. Djuna Barnes has fine hips. The Baroness now was the real stuff, the real lallypaloodle girl. She was the only one who dared to be a woman. Everything else shit (as he would say). And I'm going to be excited again and give you a whole lot for your money. First, Sherwood Anderson. I used to think a lot of him, but now I don't know. Margery is getting fat. That's why I can allow myself to feel kindly toward her. You're fat, old girl. Well, anyhow, you got a rise out of me once, but you're not an artist. Samuel Pepys, home to Florence and to bed, very ironical.

Dearest Lola, I did get started didn't I. But still I get this tremendous satisfaction, as from a blow (only sadism that ever appealed to me) in reading Bill Williams' best stuff, and always that vacuous termination because he wants to live like a drunkard and unfortunately the day after is in his books as well as the golden moment of most clear eyed delirium, and it is the day after you end with. I don't mean morally. The more gall and woodworm he can handle, the happier the effect. But, the day after in sheer stupidity and ineffectualness.

Still, he deserves more than most as an artist, and so does Waldo, who's idiotic occasionally not through any fault of nature but because he makes himself deliberately comfortable that way.

Kay also lent me this Aldous Huxley, *Antic Hay*, and there is a talent infinitely inferior to the two Americans, but still good and still about as wrong as possible. For all he is so modern, he has a real English HGWellsian mind, and has to go off into ponderous levity about social problems (just the lighter side of Wellsism) and let art stand with her hat in her hand until he notices her. I wish people in general would remember that a novel is about people, and not anything else, and that that is good in a novel which makes the people live and nothing else. I haven't remembered it with divine consistence myself. I dare say, but at least I know it ought to be remembered, and Aldous H. takes positive pride in defying it. Also he doesn't know that the satirist must create every inch of the flesh he destroys if his satire is to be telling. Well, probably no satirist ever did, but this Aldous H. needn't have made his central character quite such a hippopotamine yet non-fleshly fancy.

I'm glad Kay liked me. I liked her very much, Lola, and if I didn't rave it is because experience has begun to reach me not to rave o'ersoon in order not to curse later. I mean, I saw at once she was a sensitive, intelligent and talented girl, but just how much of a rapport for friendship that would constitute, I couldn't tell in those two days. Nor am I quite sure yet, but that I like her better and better and am more and more assured, that you, with your very penetrating prevision, have discovered somebody whose writing is going to put them in much, much more than the merely talented class. In fact, I have to wait and see whether or not she will be truly one of the great artists of her generation. I suspect she will. I have not read all her book yet, but the parts of her stuff I have seen show a sense of definition, a sense of people in their differentness as well as in their identity, that no other similar prose immediatist of her type does show. I mean she is writing in a Waldoian close-up key (sometimes beautifully and sometimes with a too hectic struggle for the evasion of the commonplace) but with this key she has a fidelity to those definitions which must emerge as differences as long as the whole of a work of art is to have parts, relations. Waldo has a fuller realisation of that one beauty of complete identity, but since he is not a lyricist and writes in dramatic terms, this one perfect value is useless for development in his present mood. He won't see the exactitude of the difference as well as the exactitude of the great stemming central identity. Well, Kay Boyle does see relations in terms that have a relational truth, as well as this other thing that allows her to speak of bread-white legs and lots of other lovely images. If she'll only hold fast and even stress this sense of the relational while she can't lose I am sure the emotional fullness under, why she'll be great. I know you have a wonderful sense of potentialities, but I had not expected her to be that good. Her admirations at present are all for the immediacy and form be damned school (I don't mean form as a subjective atmosphere) so I hope she won't kill her own advantage by stressing the turgid or the violent or the too delicate moral noncommittalness at the expense of this other thing she has. She probably won't though, since she's beginning as herself.

And if she goes where she ought −

I know Georgie O'Keefe is a real artist, but golly, Lola, I have just read Paul Rosenfeld's book and honestly and really, this piety about saving America I can't stand. I feel a desire to save your own soul by being damnably integrated and ruthlessly sincere is pardonable and right, but any body who sets out to save another fellow's soul begins with the bad taste which results in piety instead of worship. It is the piousness of the Stieglitzian group that I can't endure. By their works you shall know them, I say, and by that standard I know a lot more has been done for the prodigal (PR has this unholy romanticism about Europe) by some other people than by poor old Stieglitz. Paul R. has some fine sensings, but fumbles ultimately in such welters of adjectives, edgeless adjectives, of vague and smoky volume, and when it comes to the hallelujahs about 291, it is almost funny. But he did make me know we had missed something in not having met Randolph Bourne, and the Anderson thing, while too panegyric, too had some exquisite summings. What PR seems to do is to spoil his own effects under the Stieglitz influence. I'm thinking that the whole trouble with Waldo is still the Stieglitz effect. Stieglitz may be good for Marsden Hartley, who is so timid he will always have good taste, but I'm blamed if it is for people who have more volume and little direction of their own. Do save Kay Boyle from it. She seems to have the usual youthful feeling about that old Rabbi. His job is that of a man, half articulate himself, but sensitive, who makes other people do his articulation for him and pockets, perhaps rightly, a large part of the credit for the utterance. It was a shame Waldo wasn't in the book, and as for leaving out Paul Strand, I consider it downright indecent, for to my mind he and Martin and not your Arthur Doves et al., are the best painters I know except Sug and Merton.

Cyril spent the winter of 1924 painting in Tunisia with Elsa. His Paris exhibition sold well, and he had received public critical approval from Roger Fry and from such influential French critics as Louis Vaucelles. As a self-taught painter of two years' practice, he had every reason to feel pleased with himself.

Evelyn, Creighton and Owen Merton were at Béziers, penniless. For a time, marriage between the couple was being discussed, a prospect clouded by Merton's increasingly erratic behaviour, and the likelihood of future unrelieved poverty. There was, too, the question of his family responsibilities, a stumbling block which he was somewhat guiltily evading. At the root of his disturbed behaviour was the dilemma of choice between his mistress and his children and this could not be deferred for very much longer.

16

End of the Affair

EVELYN HAD written three unpublished books in exile: *The
Golden Door, Ideals*, a book of five satiric novelettes, and *The Grey
Riddle*. The first two were eventually published in 1925 and 1927
respectively in small editions and to poor sales. Her writing took a
radically new direction when, one evening, she and Owen went to
the cinema in Béziers to see *The Covered Wagon*, a low-budget
Hollywood saga of frontier pioneering. This had the effect of
reconciling her to the American background she had thought was
abandoned and she began work on a long book which, she
announced to Lola, promised to be in two volumes and to cover
the years from 1850 to the present. When the project was
completed six years later, it was four volumes and 2,329 pages in
length, taking in the years from the California gold migrations to
the outbreak of the First World War. Most of this was also written
in exile and drew heavily on Evelyn's own half-Southern, half-
Yankee family history. As an exercise in sustained ancestor-
worship, a Southern practice she guyed in *Background in Tennessee*, it has few equals. The immense project eventually saw
print as *Migrations* (1927), *The Wave* (1929), and the two-decker
A Calendar of Sin (1931), novels which, like the earlier trilogy,
could be read separately or as a sequence.

In early 1925 Owen Merton seemed to be undergoing a mental
crisis which Evelyn was unable to fathom and, on one occasion,
burned first his brushes, then his canvases. He left Béziers in
February of that year to prepare for his Leicester Galleries show
which was to open in March. Evelyn stayed behind with Creigh-

ton and when Cyril returned from Tunisia, left Creighton with
him at Collioure and travelled on to London where she stayed at
the Theis apartment in Temple Bar.

Collioure held for Creighton the happiest memories of his
childhood, indeed, of his life. The art colony excepted, it was still
a peasant town whose staple industry was sardine and anchovy
fishing. Like Thomas Merton, Creighton was deeply affected by
the simple fatalism of the Catholic French peasants whose
certitudes and stability he contrasted favourably with the continuous domestic chaos of his parents' lives.

More chaos loomed for Evelyn. The Leicester Galleries show
proved successful and was the peak of Owen Merton's artistic
career. It made money and, for the first time in years, he felt able
to return to see his children without cap in hand. He and Evelyn
sailed together for New York where Owen left her, and went on to
visit the Jenkinses and his children alone.

Thomas Merton remembered him as being jaunty and spor-
ting a beard which Tom insisted he remove. But beneath the
cheeriness it soon became apparent that there could be no return
to the irregular ménage of the last few years. He was faced with
two stark alternatives. He could marry Evelyn and make her
stepmother of his two children, but then he would step back into
the financial quagmire he had experienced with his first wife. Aid
from the Jenkins family would have stopped and he saw little hope
of being self-supporting. He could do little but paint and would
inevitably be forced back into the rut of menial labour to survive.
But, if he left Evelyn and assumed paternal responsibilities, he
could continue to paint and receive help from the Jenkinses.

His letters leave no doubt that he was racked by the decision
forced upon him and the summer of 1925 may have wounded him
more deeply than it did Evelyn. The eventual deciding factor was
the implacable enmity which the young Tom Merton felt toward
his potential stepmother. Writing to Lola a year after the break,
Owen explained his dilemma:

Lola, dear, will you believe my own word on the Gospel that I
know I could not have reconciled the question of the children
and the question of either living with or marrying Evelyn.
Tom's jealousy and irreconcilableness are perfectly enormous.
There was no choice except to leave the children altogether –

and then every night for the rest of my life would have been hideous with repentance – . Only I see now that for the last eighteen months I was with Evelyn, I was in a violently hysterical condition, perhaps controlling it made it more violent. Anyway, when I got to New York I saw that I could never handle the situation– Dear Lola, it would have taken two months of the most careful tact to handle the question with the Jenkins – I had failed a month before in London to keep up Evelyn's courage over the situation which I was quite certain till then that I could manage, given time – and I just busted.

After the break Owen refused to receive Evelyn's letters and, in desperation, she turned to Lola for comfort. She feared insanity and wrote a flurry of hysterical letters daily, sometimes twice daily. Owen was brutal. The Jenkins family disliked her. His refusal to defend her against them was cowardice.

It also emerged that, throughout the relationship, Owen felt that he was being unfavourably compared to Cyril. There was probably some truth in this for, when Evelyn fictionalised the triangle in *Eva Gay*, there was a sharp unflattering contrast between the mature, austere Hans Haaska and the childlike, erratic Evan Garrett. In the middle of the actual crisis Cyril offered to cable money, a gesture of generosity which in the circumstances seems close to saintliness: an offer which Evelyn had the decency to refuse.

Finally she accepted that it was over, and she returned to London and the Theis household, from where she wrote to Lola:

Yes, darling, I love *you* for writing me that Esta thinks Owen loves me. And he does, darling, but it is all very queer and messed up and maybe ruined love, if you will accept that, for what Owen has been through about Tom is as genuine as about me. Tom is a morbid and possessive kid and Owen is made morbid about Tom through various things that occurred in connection with Ruth. Tom is, and will be until he is big enough to set adrift, a constant obstacle to peace of mind. Do believe, sweetest love, (and it *is* just to Owen) he has not been light or callous or anything easily condemned. He has suffered tortures and he is weak through his impressionableness and too ready outgoing, which prevents his love for me from having an exclusive ideal quality, so that he has been made cruel and crucified on an uncontrolled capacity to feel, and not oppositely. I have no hope about anything there at present, but the deeper and deeper conviction that Owen's suffering has been as inevitable and as much to be respected, and as little to be condemned as suffering in any situation in which the emotions cannot reconcile themselves with the facts.

Owen and Tom visited Evelyn once in London, in September 1925 while en route to the South of France. 'Little Tom *hated* me. What was there to do?' she wrote despairingly. The separation was agreed to be permanent and, though Owen wrote several times in the following year, both saw no chance of reconciliation.

The brief remainder of Owen Merton's life is recounted in *The Seven Storey Mountain*. The letters written after the separation suggest that Owen still loved Evelyn; there is no record of another woman in his life before he died of a brain tumour in January 1931. His reputation as an artist, which had suffered from his nomadic, impecunious life, died with him and his strange contribution to posterity was to be a posthumous one:

I was in my room. It was night. The light was on. Suddenly it seemed to me that Father, who had now been dead more than a year, was there with me. The sense of his presence was as vivid and as real as if he had touched my arm or spoken to me. The whole thing passed in a flash, but in that flash, instantly, I was overwhelmed with a sudden and profound insight into the misery and corruption of my own soul, and I was pierced deeply with a light that made me realise something of the condition I was in, and I was filled with a strong horror at what I saw, and my whole being rose up in revolt against what was within me, and my soul desired liberation from this with an intensity and an urgency unlike anything that I had ever known.

This experience in a Rome hotel bedroom confirmed Thomas Merton on the path to Catholicism, a strange numinous illumination in which his father took the place of God. In *The Seven Storey Mountain*, the erratic, obscene, yet dedicated and unworldly Owen Merton became in recollection the ideal, strong father he might have wished to be in life.

The extremity of Thomas Merton's commitment to Catholicism was more than a simple counter-revolt against the confused circumstances of his childhood. Even as a child he shared with his father a capacity for violent outbursts and emotional anguish. He may have been aware that his father had sacrificed a possibility of happiness and perhaps the mainspring of his artistic creativity because his own jealous impulses demanded that Owen's affection be reserved for him alone. Without the discipline of the Church he, like his father, might have become 'a fumbling, brutal and fragmentary man'. And, in the absolute nature of his surrender to God, he must have hoped to reconcile the warring currents within himself, and so avoid the rocks upon which his father had so mercilessly been broken.

Evelyn stayed for several months at the Theis apartment, spending much of her time writing. 'The darn book is about as long as the Bible in eight volumes already,' she wrote to Lola, reporting on the presence in London of other American expatriates. 'I've seen Bob McAlmon who asked about you, and is unconsciously funnier 'an ever. Also met H.D., who simply HATED me, perhaps because I wrote that poem about her, and Bob's wife who looks like the virgin queen of the mosquitoes, really kind of appealing but too scared to bother with.'

Equilibrium returned to her letters. The recriminations against Owen ceased and, just before Christmas, she announced that she was leaving to spend the winter in the Scilly Isles.

On January 15, 1926 a brief letter written by Mrs John Metcalfe was sent to Lola with the conspiratorial injunction that the name change should not be made public. 'John was an effort to save my sanity.' She had been ill and was recuperating in a nursing home on this 'meagre Northern Bermuda'.

A fuller explanation followed in a letter written a fortnight later. After several pages on Owen's painting, which she was still enthusiastically promoting, and praise for Cyril's new novel, *Siren*, which had just been published in London by Faber and Gwyer, she came to the subject of her new 'husband'. She made no pretence that the affair was anything more than a rebound, necessary because of her inability to live without what she delicately termed 'a love interest'. 'Louise Theis and perhaps even Otto were a bit outraged by the "grossness" (implied) with which I went out to look for an interest [...] So I found John. Not hard to find, in the obvious sense, but he is showing himself someone upon whom affection can spend itself not just blindly for lack of object, but consciously thru a spontaneous approval. He is a year older than I am but seems younger.'

The letter conveyed little of the character of the man she was living with, who was to become her only legal husband and remain devoted to her until death. And Metcalfe himself was not given to self-revelation either in his letters or in his diaries. Except for a few occasions when, tortured by isolation, he would send out brief letters pleading for help, he was a model of reticence. Evelyn did not fictionalise him as she did several other men in her life: she remained faithful to him but, as always, in her fashion.

William John Metcalfe was born in Heacham, Norfolk, on October 6, 1891. Like Evelyn, he was an only child. His father had been a sea captain who took to religion in middle age and became a superintendent in Dr Barnardo's homes. His mother was born in India, the daughter of an Indian Army chaplain.

When he was five, his parents went to Canada to superintend a home there, returning four years later to do similar work in the East End of London. John Metcalfe was privately educated in East Anglian schools and later attended the Universities of London and Manchester. During the First World War he joined the Royal Flying Corps, an early version of the RAF, and he was still a reserve lieutenant when he met Evelyn. After the war he began schoolteaching, and started to publish his macabre stories widely in magazines, including *Outlook*.

In 1925 the best of these were collected in *The Smoking Leg*, and this book was critically and commercially successful, running to three editions. By this time both parents were dead, and he had no relatives barring an aged aunt in Salisbury. 'Très jeune in experiences,' Evelyn described him, with the implication that she was referring to the sexual and emotional sphere.

The short stories are all explorations of the sinister and a sense of near-supernatural darkness pervades the novels also. The horror is more psychological than occult and the books, like their author, are exercises in suggestion. The creaking machinery of the Gothic mode is completely absent. The books offer few clues to understanding the man. Two of the novels, *Arm's Length* and *Spring Darkness*, have an almost identical theme: the passion felt by a stiff and proper young man of the lower middle class for a girl who is several rungs below him socially. The world they depict is a seedy down-at-heel milieu, either in the London suburbs or in provincial seaside resorts. They are extremely English.

A distinctive, recurrent feature of the fictions is whisky consumption, and in the few accounts of Metcalfe given by friends, his fondness for a good malt is often alluded to. The main character in *All Friends Are Strangers*, a novel published just after the Second World War, suffers an alcoholically induced breakdown. Metcalfe seems to have turned heavily to drink in his troubled later years, but whether he had a lifelong drink problem is nowhere alluded to by himself or Evelyn. Nor, strangely, is the fact that he was prone to epilepsy.

If the fictions accurately reflect Metcalfe's inner world, it must have been a peculiarly hellish one. He was a strange choice of lifelong partner for Evelyn in many ways, since he corresponded neither to the surrogate father represented by Cyril, nor the confused child whose lover/mother she became in her involvements with Owen and Waldo. But both shared the loneliness of the only child, a tendency to sickness and invalidity and a degree of mental imbalance which was to assert itself more strongly as they grew older together. Beside the few known details of his life and the clues to be gleaned from his fictions, John Metcalfe remains a mystery. Apart from his work, the man cast no shadow.

Cyril spent the winter in Tunisia with Elsa and Creighton, who remembered school there as being even worse than Algeria had been. The school was so rough that eventually he had to be withdrawn. The schoolmistress had gone about armed with a dried bull's penis which she used as a weapon to ward off schoolboy tormentors.

Cyril was doing well. Elsa was of independent means, his painting was selling and he still received an allowance from Marie Garland. As usual Evelyn was penniless, but when she and John returned to London from the Scilly Isles, she sent a draft of *Migrations* to her American agent. From somewhere she and John found the money to meet the Tunisian party at Marseilles in June 1926 and, taking Creighton, they found a flat in Cassis sur Mer.

The flat was small and the town expensive and overrun with tourists. They stayed for only a few months, but it was here that Evelyn began a long-standing friendship with one of the most remarkable women of her time.

17

The Third Colour

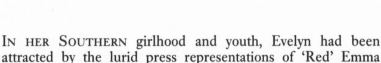

IN HER SOUTHERN girlhood and youth, Evelyn had been attracted by the lurid press representations of 'Red' Emma Goldman very largely because Evelyn's railroad executive father regarded her as a serious public menace. Emma had been in the forefront of the anarchist movement for two decades and its most inspired orator before a nervous government deported her to Soviet Russia in 1919 as an alien agitator. The two women had no chance to meet in New York, though they had many common friends including Ellen Kennan and Lola Ridge, who had been a contributor to Emma's magazine *Mother Earth*. It was perhaps inevitable that the two rebel exiles in Europe would somehow be drawn together.

Emma's autobiography, *Living My Life*, records the first meeting as having taken place in London; if so, it must have been brief. But at Cassis a friendship began which was to last until Emma's death fourteen years later. Like the long friendships with Kay Boyle and Lola Ridge, the relationship rested in an intense correspondence and the two women crossed paths infrequently. It was an unlikely friendship for, though Evelyn was sympathetic toward individualism, almost all political activity lacked the absolute values which she admired in life. Evelyn made her position clear in the first letter to Emma when, commenting on the British General Strike, she remarked: 'I feel sympathetic to the men who are individual participants, but the English labor leaders don't fire me with enthusiasm. It is the supposed – and perhaps actual – "necessity" for unlovely compromise that, for me, robs the whole business of guts, and, for all but the few elect who are martyrs, leaves art as the only full outlet. It is your attitude toward your beliefs that I admire and always will. There aren't many like you.' In the same letter she confessed: 'I think you'll be willing to accept me as I am, so you will realise that I have somewhere lost what I once thought I had – the temperament for an ideal devotion to the cause you have given so much for.'

Emma Goldman was twenty-four years older than Evelyn, a stocky and unbeautiful figure who, however, was still capable of arousing passion in men much younger than herself. Like the Mother Earth of the magazine she founded, her appeal was maternal and it was her generous spirit more than her ideas which gained her a following. Creighton specifically excluded her from his blanket condemnation of his mother's friends with the observation that the worst he had heard of her was that her sympathies were so large, they often seemed indiscriminate.

Ideologically she followed Kropotkin and the so-called communist anarchist line, though her initial enthusiasm for the Russian Revolution soon faded and was entirely extinguished by Trotsky's brutal suppression of the Kronstadt sailors. She never saw in Trotsky a symbol of the Revolution betrayed and in 1932, after he was cast into exile, she wrote to Evelyn, 'True, Trotsky deserves all he gets. He was the last to show the least mercy to any of his opponents.'

By 1921 both she and her comrade in exile, Alexander Berkman, were vocally critical of the direction which the Revolution was taking, and in 1923 Emma expressed these criticisms in a book, *My Disillusionment in Russia*. At this stage the Great Romance between the Soviet experiment and Western intelligentsia had scarcely begun and John Reed's starry-eyed effusions were the main text by a sympathetic outsider on the way in which the world was being shaken.

Unlike Reed, Emma was a native Russian. More importantly, she had already reached an evolved political position from which she could pass judgement. She regarded the individual as being of paramount importance; she was a libertarian first and a communist second. From being a critical observer of the Soviet experiment, her position hardened through the twenties and thirties to one of implacable anti-Sovietism. It was a stance which Evelyn came to adopt, partly as a result of Emma's influence, as the strength of the Communist Party grew in the New York intelligentsia. The communists despised the anarchists: Lenin had dismissed communist anarchism as an infantile disorder. And there were no friends on the other side, for J. Edgar Hoover, who was instrumental in Emma's deportation, never lost the conviction that anarchism was as great a threat to the American way as communism.

Its threat long predated that of communism. In 1892 Alexander Berkman, who was then Emma's lover, had disastrously misapplied the methods of the Russian nihilists and shot Henry Clay Frick, chairman of Carnegie Steel and symbol of the brutality of American corporate capitalism. At that time Carnegie Steel was engaged in a bitter struggle against unionisation and all workers except blacklegs were locked out. Though disarrayed groupings of socialists protested, it was left to the anarchists to effect propaganda by the deed.

The affair was a miserable and tragic failure on all counts. Berkman first constructed a time bomb, which failed to go off, then decided on a revolver as his weapon. After the farcical episode of Emma's attempted venture into prostitution to raise money for the weapon, graphically recounted in *Living My Life*, Berkman confronted Frick in his Pittsburg office and shot three times. In spite of the nearly point-blank range, Frick was no more than slightly wounded. Berkman was captured and a half-hearted attempt at suicide frustrated when a phial of fulminate of mercury was forcibly removed from his mouth. After the brief formality of a trial he was sentenced to twenty-one years in prison.

The steelworkers' union on whose unbidden behalf Berkman had acted was a conservative body whose members, for the most part, wanted no truck with anarchism. Their quarrel with Frick had begun as a wage dispute and had escalated into a question of union recognition. Abstract notions of distributive justice had little appeal or interest to them and Berkman's act was incomprehensible to the majority of steelworkers. Frick basked in the public sympathy accorded to victims of assassination attempts and, shortly afterward, the strike was broken. When Berkman's former mentor, Johann Most, repudiated the action, Emma publicly attacked him with a horsewhip and the already divided anarchist movement collapsed.

When Berkman was released in 1907, Emma Goldman had

become the figurehead of American anarchism and a force in the worlds of political and literary radical thought. The years of imprisonment had destroyed any physical passion between the couple, but they remained together until Berkman's death in 1936. Until their expulsion to Russia they crusaded through *Mother Earth*, and through Emma's impassioned oratory, for a whole range of radical causes. Several attempts were made to incriminate them and, in the eyes of the press and the law, there were few outrages in which they were not somehow implicated.

The hardening of the Russian Revolution into a new autocracy was for both a second loss of political innocence. Emma had abandoned advocacy of political violence after the Frick débâcle, and if her repudiation was sometimes equivocal this was only because Berkman had suffered years of imprisonment for his act. To Evelyn, whose connection with anarchism was tenuous and whose sympathies were outside practical politics, Emma would confess further disillusionments which she might have concealed from more committed friends. Evelyn's encouragement gave Emma much of the necessary energy to complete *Living My Life*, and a great deal of reassurance besides this when Emma despaired of the world. She was at home on the platform and in the worlds of literary and political criticism, but her letters show that she found the re-living necessary to write her autobiography an enormous strain. Evelyn's influence might conceivably account for the absence of ideology in the book. *Living My Life* is an immensely readable and entertaining memoir, but the reader learns little of the precise beliefs underpinning a lifetime of activism.

These beliefs were subject to hard knocks in the course of events. Writing to Evelyn on the Sacco and Vanzetti verdicts, Emma was pessimistic and saw no improvement in American public attitudes since the Haymarket martyrs' hangings in 1887: 'But the Sacco and Vanzetti conspiracy convinced me that all my efforts over the period of a lifetime were in vain,' she complained. 'But then it was not only the State of Massachusetts which killed Sacco and Vanzetti – it was the entire United States, the vast bulk of indolent, self-satisfied, crassly materialistic mass which cares only for its own insatiable appetites for food and joy, and has no interest or feeling for the dreadful things that happened in its midst.'

She took heart from Sacco and Vanzetti themselves and from the groups who went to Boston to protest. She was taken aback when Evelyn dismissed the protests as futile and the killings a mere drop in the ocean of crimes committed by law against individuals every day. The struggle to write the autobiography was another source of pessimistic judgements and in June 1928 Emma wrote: 'I want very much to have the memoirs done by June 1929. That year will have deep meaning for me. In the first place I will have rounded out sixty years – certainly the largest part of one's life. And I will have given forty years to my ideas. I realise that most of them were spent chasing windmills, in trying to present to the world an ideal which to me contains all the beauty and wonder there is in life. The only *raison d'être* for my existence, and the world less than ever wants to know about it. You can imagine I would despair utterly if I did not believe in the ultimate triumph of my ideal.'

In the letters, it was often Evelyn who radiated hope in the future of anarchism while Emma became more despondent as, with the onset of the Depression, the popularity of Soviet Russia rose. Emma admitted to Eliot White in 1931 that Bolshevism was much worse than Tsarism and her influence confirmed Evelyn's anti-communism; a stance which, after an unpleasant confinement with a group of communist fanatics at Yaddo, the writers' and artists' retreat, needed little encouragement. After this encounter she wrote in August 1931: 'The one authentic value of "manners", as I see it, is that they presume mutual respect for personality. It would be better not to have them formulated, but I am dead against the complete contempt for individuality which seems to go with the kind of thought which is sympathetic as it concerns itself with cures for economic justice. I am always finding myself between the black and the white and having it disputed that there can be a third colour. You know what independence costs.'

A letter written a few weeks later expressed the increasing isolation of her position: 'And individualists like myself – incurable believers in what has now become démodé as a "romantic" movement– are caught between the Scilla of bourgeois obtuseness and the Charibdis of a radicalism that rejects appeal on the only grounds that are moving and arresting to people who love a free spirit. For this reason one is thrown back on oneself in a fashion very disastrous to one's natural love of life.'

Her opposition to communism was from a libertarian, not a conservative standpoint. In her New Orleans adolescence she had been 'three quarters Marxist' but, as increasing numbers of her friends sought salvation of Moscow, her anti-communism became obsessive. The communists in the early thirties were a small, vocal minority in the literary world but Evelyn found them to be fanatical, ungenerous and personally unattractive from the outset: 'The Communists, as I meet them in America, though they do not realise it, have much the attitude of revivalists at a camp meeting. Come on brother and get right with god, or go to hell! There's all the emotionalism of conversion, with an accent stress as to the damnation of the capitalist infidel, but, beyond the conversion they don't see. The lust to destroy seems to them holy, and holy it may be when the provocation is great. But I don't see any splendid future, such as they believe in, arising from a program which, when you boil it down, has only negative canons of belief.'

In the early thirties Evelyn suggested that Emma and Berkman should make a concerted effort to re-enter America, but this prospect seemed absurdly unrealistic to Emma. Berkman had experienced a succession of visa problems in France and only narrowly avoided expulsion in 1931. Emma was safer as, by virtue of a marriage of convenience to James Colton, a radical collier, she was a British passport holder. In August 1933 she wrote Evelyn a letter revealing her deep pessimism on that issue, and on the general drift of American political life:

Darling Evelyn, you are naive indeed to think that the time will ever come to make our return to America possible. There is no hope whatever for Sasha (Berkman). And there is damned little for me. Not even if I had people in the states who have the will and the way of starting a campaign to bring me back. Besides, there is no one. As to any fundamental change in America that would open her gates to us. Really dearest, I marvel at your naivety. Witness how the American people have fallen for the Roosevelt bait. How they always grab at every straw and the coat tails of every soothseer. What hope is there in such a people or such a country that so completely lacks its own mind, its ability to think out any proposition to its logical conclusion?

You are right of course when you say that a Communist change would only be a bloody mess. But that too, because no one thinks for himself. Everyone wants to be led, whether it be from the Left or from the Right. The American Intelligentsia is among the worst lick spittles. They have all fallen for Russia as the promised land. While the masses hang on to Roosevelt for dear life, I ask you what chances for us? No my dearest, there is no hope. It is only that you permit your wish to be father to your thought that you can see revolutionary signs in America. True, I am not on the spot, and perhaps I should not judge. But I keep in touch with events. And more important still is the fact that 15 million unemployed have done nothing these three years to take matters in their own hands.

You will say, and you will be right, that people everywhere have remained in cowardly submission to their masters. They have not lifted a finger to help themselves. The deeper the tragedy of those who had some faith in the masses.

Both the masses and the intelligentsia appeared, as the thirties progressed, to confirm this pessimistic prognosis. However, her pessimism was less well grounded on the inflexibility of the United States, and the following year she was granted a ninety-day visa, for which Evelyn actively lobbied the State Department, in order to give a lecture tour.

This was not an over-all success. It was boycotted by the communists and Nazi sympathisers and, in Emma's absence, the anarchist movement had crumbled, largely for the lack of a charismatic figurehead of her stature. It had failed to mobilise a new generation of radicals since, unlike the Communist Party, it could not point to a paradise in the making. The movement had been reduced to its original constituency of immigrant Jews and Italians and Emma found herself delivering many of her lectures in Yiddish. After the tour, Evelyn wrote to Emma commiserating over its apparent failure:

About the New York lectures, I think the Communist boycott may have been a greater influence than you know. New York is the one place where the 'intelligentsia' are a paramount influence in the success or failure of public events. I am not the definitely political target you are, but you might be amazed to know how much in my difficulties has been accentuated by Communist dislike. You see as a writer I am in measure a skeptic. This is not the failure of my ideals, but it is due to my feeling that achievement will be sounder when all potential self-deceptions and disillusions have been faced. The literary world of New York at least is engulfed in a Salvation Army feeling about the Communist movement and as this is nine-tenths emotional only (a gesture of despair as you have pointed out), very few have the guts to endure any criticalness whatsoever. So the skepticism which I think should be concurrent with positive effort to eradicate its causes is regarded, when applied to Communist types, Communist leaders, a Communist party at all, as the foulest treachery to the masses [...] Anarchy requires of all men the spirit which makes leaders. Communism attracts only (no, I won't say only – but largely) those who like best to be led with as much sound and fury and little individual responsibility and thought.

In spite of her distrust of the Party Evelyn retained the friendship of numerous fellow-travellers. Theodore Dreiser, a girlhood hero of hers with whom she maintained an irregular correspondence, was courted by the communists and appeared on several front-organisation platforms. He was, however, too idiosyncratic to be subjected to a line and was soon abandoned as being more trouble than he was worth. His support of rebellion was indiscriminate; in 1931 he contributed to a fund set up for Emma and personally appealed to Laval that Berkman should not be expelled from France. But Floyd Dell, one of the Village crowd of the twenties, refused to contribute to the fund, citing Emma's anti-Sovietism as a reason. Party influence in the literary world was strong among critics and editors rather than artists, many of whom showed a disconcerting penchant for independence. The Party line required some mental agility to be followed to the letter and, on occasion, generated some fine absurdities. After the Hitler–Stalin pact, one eminent New York critic and Party sympathiser actually entertained a visiting group of Hitler Youth in his apartment. In such a climate the anarchist perspective, far from being Utopian and idealistic, takes on an air of solid common sense.

The two women were united on more than the questions of

individualism and anti-communism, since both were believers in
the principle of free love. Evelyn's letters attack the institution of
marriage yet, strangely, she kept up a pretence of being married
to men to whom she was not. Both remained close to the men
they had first loved for much of their lives, though in both cases
sexual relations had ceased. After a letter in which Emma spoke
of her devotion to Berkman, Evelyn wrote: 'I think I do know
something of your feeling in parallel in that I have never in a
deeply human sense cared more for anybody in the world than
Cyril and never shall; and I too feel baffled in my desire to make
his life easier as some return for the deepest of all debts I owe to
him.'

And both could be temperamental and difficult women.
When, in 1933, Evelyn canvassed Lola Ridge's support for the
proposal to admit Emma to America, she had forgotten that the
two women had quarrelled some years earlier. She later apologised for the request: 'She has been a good friend to me, but that
is a matter of getting off with the foot which happened not to step
on her corns.' So many of Evelyn's friendships ended in mutual
bitterness that it is surprising that these two prima donnas
maintained their relationship without a break. Apart from her
encouragement, Emma respected Evelyn's sharp critical intelligence which, though sympathetic to her cause, was not one of a
camp-follower. The fact that the friendship was conducted by
letter was no bar, certainly on Evelyn's part, to the possibility of a
serious dispute. But the rift never occurred.

For both women, 1936 was a trying year. Berkman committed
suicide in Nice after a painful prostate operation and Emma was
shattered. In England John Metcalfe, after a series of physical
illnesses, underwent a serious mental breakdown.

Emma threw herself into involvement with the anarchist
faction in the Spanish Civil War and what was to be the last
disillusionment of her political career. In America, Evelyn began
to canvass the intelligentsia in the hope of mobilising the political
'third colour', but by this time polarisation had gone too far and
the replies she received were, at best, equivocal.

Emma blamed the rout of anarchist forces in Spain squarely
on Soviet interference. Yet she could not abandon the idea of
revolution as the decisive, transcendent force which would
deliver the masses to freedom. In a long letter written in 1938 in

response to Evelyn's enquiry as to her position on communism, she outlined her theory fully:

The frightful contagion of communism has brought about changes in the people one never thought possible. Men and women but yesterday who were friends have become the most raving enemies; but it is also true that many who repudiated everything one had to say in criticism of the regime in Russia have come to see the light, and have come to appreciate what Alexander Berkman and myself wrote and said in 1921 [...]

Dearest Evelyn – we don't have to argue about the efficacy of revolution. Judging from the events in Russia and in Spain, you are undoubtedly right in your stand. I myself am not quite sure whether revolutions bring the desired relief, or whether it is not in their nature to end up in dictatorship, untold suffering and war to defend what the revolution was meant to realise; but on the other hand I do not see how else the masses will ever bring about fundamental changes. To be sure reforms, changes of a superficial nature, in the way of social insurance, better hours and a number of other such things need no revolution. The only trouble is that these reforms make the masses more satisfied with their lot – more contented with what their organisations and leaders are doing for them. England is a case in point. Since my first visit to this country in 1896, and now after considerable changes have taken place in the status of the workers, economic, politically and educationally etc, whatever revolutionary spirit or libertarian longing the workers of this country may have had in the past have gone by the board. They have been placed in the grip of the Labour Party – Trades Unions and the rest. They are completely dominated by their leaders and have not the desire or strength to stand up for anything better than was handed down to them from on top. In other words they have become a static mass – more difficult to move than 40 years ago or more.

Now it is quite true that revolutions uproot everything and everybody; but also its effects are far reaching and fundamental. Even Russia where the Soviet regime has been mowing down everything in its way and the Russian masses have been put in a new strait-jacket, the revolution has left its indelible

mark on the masses of the Russian people, and it is even more
so in the case of Spain. In point of truth, the Spanish revolution, regardless of the horrors of war and the cruel result of
the German and Italian support of Franco, goes marching on.
Even if Franco and his German and Italian supporters should
triumph, they will not eradicate from the Spanish people their
revolutionary fibre – their very deep ground longing for
freedom. So you see my dear – while I realise the heartbreak-
ing effects of revolutions – I nevertheless feel that they are
worthwhile provided they are not imposed from the top –
provided they arise from the bowels of the earth, or the masses
themselves.

But why argue – to me our friendship is so deep and so
strong that we can continue to differ on certain points. That
will never destroy my love for you and I am sure it will not you
for me.

When Emma sealed the file of her letters to and from Evelyn,
she wrote on it, 'Correspondence with Evelyn Scott, America's
foremost writer': a judgement which says more about the depth of
feeling between the two women and the influence each had on the
other's judgement than it says about Emma's critical perspicacity.
Her politics may have been utopian and programmed to failure in
the face of the closed ranks which opposed her, but Emma
Goldman's achievement cannot be assessed on that basis alone.
Her anarchism was the philosophical base from which she made
real contributions in the practical fields of feminism and birth
control. As a left-wing critic of the aberrations of the God that
failed, she is a more reliable commentator than the apostates who
once believed, then recanted, and infinitely more reliable than the
Stalin that failed, Leon Trotsky, the butcher of Kronstadt. The
bedrock of her philosophy was a respect for the individual, and
this belief never faltered though all her other ideas were sorely
tested by the course of events. Her last publication, before she
died in Toronto in 1940, was a pamphlet, *The Place of the
Individual in Society*, an affirmation that this tenet still held firm.

Individualism had been a cornerstone of twenties radicalism
but was at a particularly low premium in the polarised, hysterical
atmosphere of thirties politics. If Emma's statements and actions
seem to contain several contradictions, it is because they come

from an individual capable of self-questioning, not from a party dictate or slavish adherence to a line. And, judged as an individual, it is difficult not to feel a great deal of warmth for Emma Goldman.

18
The Crest of
The Wave

IN LATE 1926 Evelyn, John, Cyril and Creighton left Cassis for a winter of travelling together. Spain laid the whole group low with stomach complaints and they soon left for Portugal where Evelyn and Cyril's fluency in the language proved useful. Elsa, meanwhile, had returned to Switzerland to look after her sick mother.

Evelyn's letters of this period radiate little sense of place. Mentally she was delving into her own family background, which she had quarried successfully for *Migrations*. The sequel, provisionally called *The Net*, was to encompass almost every facet of the Civil War in an episodic form, with no plot or central character to unite it. 'It has nearly a hundred characters and will be five hundred pages long. Do you guess I will ever be able to publish it?' she asked Lola, to whom the finished book would be dedicated.

The Wave, when complete, had more than a hundred characters and ran to 625 pages of densely packed prose. It was Evelyn's greatest critical and commercial success and restored her reputation, which had flagged after so long an exile. It was partly responsible for a fashion for big books on the Civil War which reached its peak with Margaret Mitchell's *Gone with the Wind* in 1936. Evelyn reviewed this book for *The Nation* and, though she gave qualified approval, she found the romantic Southern moonlight and nostalgia for the Lost Cause difficult to take.

Objectivity was a keynote of *The Wave*, stemming from a half-Southern, half-Yankee background which, on both sides, had spent the duration of the Civil War getting rich. So impartial was the book that, when Ellen Glasgow was preparing an essay on Southern writers, she had to make private enquiries whether Evelyn was a Southerner. A Northerner, Robert Frost, was incensed by what he saw as 'ineffably old-South feminine snobbish dirt' in her portrayal of General Grant. 'American history shouldn't be written by women novelists with English sympathies for the arrogant old slave-holding days,' he concluded in a sentence which casts doubt on whether he had ever read the book.

The Wave might have received a good deal of Marxist critical support, had its author been a communist. Though major historical personages interweave the narrative, it is largely a people's history of the war and its effects, which stretch as far as Manchester textile workers made jobless because of the cotton shortage. And its view of history as a process to which all members of society are integrally subject is wholly Marxist but, at a time when a Marxist novel was one written by a Party member, such niceties were lost. The lack of a central character makes *The Wave* demanding reading; doubly so if the subject matter does not grip the reader. However, it could well lay claim to be the ultimate Civil War novel and arguably the greatest war novel to have been written by a woman. In the mid-fifties, when Evelyn was trying to rekindle her literary career, Caroline Gordon offered to write the introduction for a reprint. This was a generous gesture as she had written a Civil War novel herself and more was involved than the solidarity of one Clarksville girl with another down on her luck, but nothing came of the project.

This very American novel was written in the south of France, a Portuguese hotel, an Algerian oasis town, the Hollywood Hotel in Montreal and sundry points between. The years 1926 to 1928 involved a great deal of travelling for Evelyn and John, with no apparent purpose beyond somewhere cheap and warm to write. Occasionally Evelyn solicited information from an American correspondent to verify a fact, but the actual historical recreation took place *in absentia*.

Evelyn visited America briefly from Montreal and had a serious quarrel, later patched up, with the proud, invalid Lola Ridge. Evelyn had started a fund to send Lola to a rural sanatorium where she could write and recover from a tubercular complaint.

When she learned of this Lola insisted that all the money, several hundred dollars, be returned to the donors. Montreal was enlivened by a reunion with Emma Goldman, but Evelyn did not like the city much. She and John remained there, he working as a schoolteacher, pending his being allowed into America on the quota system. Eventually he was granted entry and for a while worked as a barge captain on the East River; a popular job among hard-up writers.

By 1928, Cyril had also returned to America with Creighton, and in New York he learned of the death of Elsa. This shock, and the strain of city life on his weak heart, determined him to seek a healthier climate. Accompanied by Creighton he travelled to the Southwest to visit his old patron, Marie Garland, who had built a huge house half-way between Taos and Santa Fé. They stayed here for several months, while Cyril pondered on the next move.

Inexplicably he decided to regularise his common law 'marriage' with Evelyn by getting a divorce, which he did on March 16, 1928 in Juarez, Mexico. A Mexican divorce was something of a joke and, since there was no legal marriage, his motives are beyond speculation. In 1919, the year the Scotts returned to America, the US Treasury Department published *A Digest of the Law relating to Common Law Marriage in the States*, a document which attempted to clarify various court judgements on the question. Common law marriages were certainly not valid in Louisiana, but they seemed to have some validity in about half of the States, including New York. The divorce document gives no date of marriage, and the only straightforward thing is the grounds: desertion of bed and board.

Evelyn had called herself Mrs Metcalfe for two years by this time and insisted on her return to America that it be known that she and John were married. In future she would sometimes say she married Metcalfe in 1925, when they began living together, sometimes in 1928 when her divorce became effective and sometimes in 1930 when the couple went through a legal ceremony in Tierra Amarillo. By this time Cyril had thrown up a fresh smokescreen by hyphenating his last two names to become Cyril Kay-Scott, a usage which, he weakly asserted in his memoir, had become current during his years in Europe.

Having divorced, he decided to begin yet another career, this time as a teacher of art. He also embarked on another marriage,

with Phyllis Crawford, a sometime writer for the *New Yorker* who
had followed him out West. He set up an art school with the
remains of his money in Santa Fé, a town which boasted the
largest number of serious resident artists per head of population
in the Western hemisphere. With a new name, a new wife and a
new profession, he seemed to have fallen on his feet once more.

But he had reckoned without the jealousy of his patron, Marie
Garland. It seems probable that she was once his mistress as well
as patron to both him and Evelyn. She and Evelyn disliked each
other and she took exception to Evelyn's replacement by another
woman whom she also disliked. The twenty-five dollar weekly
allowance which both had received was abruptly terminated,
precipitating a financial crisis in New York, where Evelyn was
awaiting publication of *The Wave*, and more seriously in Santa Fé.

Cyril had borrowed heavily to found a summer art school at El
Paso, and a permanent school at Santa Fé. Without the allowance, it seemed that imminent bankruptcy faced him before he
had begun either. At a low ebb in El Paso, exhausted by overwork
and completely impoverished, he stayed in the boarding house
belonging to the mother of a man who, many years later, would
expend much time and energy unravelling the mystery of his
mother's former lodger.

On February 25, 1929 Evelyn wrote to Emma Goldman that *The
Wave* had been sold. The sale averted the worst financial crisis
since Brazil and the book was to be the first American publication
by a new firm, Jonathan Cape and Harrison Smith.

Evelyn wrote a three-hundred-page children's book, *Witch
Perkins*, in six weeks of solid writing, then began work on *Blue
Rum*, a boy's adventure yarn eventually published under the
pseudonym of Ernest Souza. She later confessed that it was
written purely for money and with one eye on possible sales in
Hollywood. The latter possibility remained just that but, whatever her motives, it was the best juvenile she wrote and an unusual
book to have been written by a woman. It has no prominent
female characters and is an adventure yarn in the style of John
Buchan or E. Phillips Oppenheim, drawing on the real-life
finding of the Cercadinho diamond. It sold well, especially in
France, but not well enough to tempt her into that fiction market
again. *Blue Rum* was the only lapse in her views on the sacred

nature of the word and the undesirability of prostituting her
literary gifts. (In 1924 she was offered a large sum by *Cosmopolitan*
to write an abridgement of *Escapade* in language more suited to
the mass market. She rejected the offer with horror though, at the
time, the money would have been very useful.)

When *The Wave* was published to good sales and critical
acclaim, Evelyn found herself in the rare position of being on
good terms with her publisher, Harrison Smith. He gave her the
manuscript of a novel by William Faulkner, a Mississippi author
who had published three earlier books which received little
recognition from critics or the public. The book was *The Sound
and the Fury*.

Themes of madness in the context of decaying Southern
grandeur were close to Evelyn's own experience and she wrote
Smith a long enthusiastic letter praising the book in superlative
terms which would not become current in Faulkner criticism for
decades to come. Her comments were so perceptive that the
publishers issued the letter in pamphlet form with the foreword:

> This essay by Evelyn Scott, whose recent novel *The Wave*
> placed her among the outstanding literary figures of her time,
> has been printed in this form and is being distributed to those
> who are interested in Miss Scott's work and the writing of
> William Faulkner. *The Sound and the Fury* should place William
> Faulkner in company with Evelyn Scott.

The irony of these words was lost to the world in 1949 when, as
Faulkner received the Nobel Prize, Evelyn Scott was a forgotten
woman living close to starvation in London. Strangely, after this
initial enthusiasm, she did not follow up her perceptions in a more
sustained way. There is no record of any meeting with Faulkner,
or of correspondence between the two writers. However, when
Faulkner was asked by Don Brennan in the summer of 1940
whether there were any good women writers, he replied, 'Well,
Evelyn Scott was pretty good, for a woman ... '

As there were a number of other women novelists he might
have named, this must have been more than a belated recognition
of her early tribute. The novels of both shared a common
preoccupation with violence, neurosis and disease and there is
much in Evelyn's fiction, the historical trilogy especially, with

which Faulkner would have identified. Given the mutual admiration, it is doubly surprising that there was no contact between them.

Evelyn used the success of *The Wave* to inveigle her publisher to print a book of verse. *The Winter Alone* came out in 1930 to an almost unanimous critical mauling and only Lola Ridge commended it. Evelyn retorted, characteristically, that because she had been pigeonholed as a prose writer, critics couldn't accept that she could write verse. But they were right and she was wrong: the embryonic talent she had shown in *Precipitations* had been stillborn.

In 1929 Evelyn and John made a brief visit to England and, on their return, decided to join Cyril and Creighton in the Southwest. Friends in New York warned that this would inevitably lead to complications but Evelyn ignored them and, at the height of summer after a long overland journey, the couple arrived at Santa Fé.

19

Way Out West - 1

THE HISTORY of art colonies in the south-western states reached its peak with the relatively brief, eighty-week residence of D. H. Lawrence in and around the Mable Dodge Luhan circus at Taos. The farce and petty jealousy surrounding this event found a pale echo in the activities of other artists and writers who had made their homes in the region. Gossip and intrigue abounded, as did emotional tangles which would have amazed the solid citizens of the states of New Mexico and Colorado, had they been privy to the innermost secrets of the settlers' lives. As the Paris twenties were largely 'Greenwich Village goes to Europe', the Taos–Santa Fé axis was the same phenomenon gone West. Lawrence soon left, but not before providing material for a number of books of reminiscences on his stay, the writing of which was to be a minor cottage industry for Taosenos for decades to come.

Though Lawrence was dying in Europe as Evelyn and John arrived, Mrs Luhan still presided at Taos and many of the main actors were still in evidence. The poet Witter Bynner was one, and in the 1929 prospectus of his art school Cyril listed him as a member of the advisory board and lecturer on Chinese poetry and painting. Bynner was the closest friend Evelyn made while out West and she maintained a correspondence with him until the early fifties. He was a waspish homosexual poet of a minor order whose main claims to the attention of posterity rest on two spiteful acts. The first was the Spectra hoax perpetrated on Alfred Kreymborg, in which Bynner was the prime mover. The second was the publication in 1951 of what is generally ranked as the most unpleasant memoir of Lawrence, *Journey with Genius*, a book whose title belies its venomous content. None the less, he must have had personal charm, for he remained a long-time friend of both Evelyn and Lawrence.

Before moving West, Mabel Dodge had been the most notorious hostess of the New York modern movement in her salon at 23 Fifth Avenue. Many of the Village crowd, including John Reed, a former lover, and Emma Goldman, had been entertained there, and some of these too had made their way out West. Among them was Ida Rauh who had acted – badly by all accounts – the part of Carroll Lamont, Evelyn's alter ego, in the Provincetown Players' production of *Love*. Ida Rauh was then married to the radical Max Eastman and later married artist Andrew Dasburg, who was also an adviser to Cyril's school.

For a year-old institution, the prospectus of the Santa Fé Art School was impressive. With an eye to political realities, Cyril had co-opted the Senator, State Governor and Mayor on to his advisory panel, as well as a cross-section of the most noteworthy local painters. He also succeeded in having the school incorporated in the civic educational system and it was located, rent-free, within the city hall itself. The prospectus laid heavy emphasis on sound technique and contained a long list of commendations on Cyril's work from critics, including Roger Fry and Alfred Stieglitz. It also stated that 'Mr Kay-Scott has taught over a long period abroad'.

In spite of the fact that this claim was a huge extension of the facts, the school was successful. A great deal of bitchery and in-fighting went on, alluded to, but never clarified, in letters of the time, though no attempted palace revolution toppled Cyril.

He was quickly struck by the contrast between the 'tepid Bohemian sophistication' of the artist settlers and the rugged tradition which still flourished at the end of the Santa Fé trail. He had been born in Missouri, at the beginning of that trail and, though he had affinities with both worlds, belonged fully to neither. Perhaps this was why he made his school succeed where others had failed. Creighton seems, for a time, to have embraced redneck values; he wore a Stetson, carried a knife, and wrote lurid letters to Lola Ridge indicating that, in his mind at least, the Indian Wars were still being fought.

And the landscape was magnificent: mountains and boundless

desert dotted with prehistoric remains, Indian villages and Spanish settlements which contributed a unique colonial architecture. 'You would love this country. Half of it hangs in the sky,' Evelyn wrote to Lola and, years later, she would recall New Mexico as the most beautiful of all places she had ever lived.

Her initial impressions of Cyril's new wife were good, but that was often how things began. She had not, she insisted to Lewis Gannett, come West to set up a ménage à trois; in fact she denied ever having lived in one, 'as such arrangements are conventionally defined'. She had come to be closer to Creighton, now an adolescent, and she and Cyril decided to make his future more secure by investing in land. As with all Evelyn's investments, this turned out badly and the land was eventually sold at a loss.

Typically, John's impressions of Santa Fé remain unrecorded. Since meeting Evelyn he had published two novels, *Spring Darkness* and *Arm's Length*. Both were well received in England, especially the former which received a laudatory review from Cyril Connolly in the *New Statesman*. In America they drew a blank, which demonstrated to Metcalfe that his highly individual, quintessentially English talent was not for export. Indeed, it is difficult to see how these exercises in suburban macabre could have found favour in an America reeling from the Wall Street collapse. Evelyn's novels were similarly disregarded in England, where sales of *The Wave* throughout the British Empire totalled 380. Other novels she published in England would sometimes receive good notices, but sales were invariably insignificant.

Metcalfe must have felt himself an alien in America. He was jobless in Santa Fé and though he sold two stories to *Scribner's Magazine* his income from writing was limited. These factors caused him to make a fateful decision to ship out on a cargo boat to Columbia for a few months. On this uncomfortable voyage he contracted a dose of amoebic dysentery, a debilitating and socially embarrassing complaint which was to plague him for many years to come.

In his absence Evelyn forged on with the third volume of her historical trilogy, *A Calendar of Sin*, which covered American history from the reconstruction after the Civil War down to 1914 in a massive sweep which closely paralleled the stories of the Thomas and Dunn families. She described it as 'the sexual and financial drama of America', and subtitled it 'American Melodramas'. Sexual repression was the key to the drama, and Clifton Fadiman was to observe that the book rested on the idea 'that murder, rape, self-mutilation, sadism and suicide were the necessary products of any society which systematically distorted its erotic energies'.

It was more cohesive than *The Wave* but, when published in 1931, its enormous length and complex construction prevented it from achieving the near-popular success of that book. Though much of the story was based on Evelyn's family history, one wholly fictional element was added. This was the rape and subsequent murder of an adolescent girl, Edith, by a Negro. The girl's circumstances and history clearly parallel Evelyn's own adolescence. This episode, and a combined murder and suicide, close the book. It is not difficult to see why she and Faulkner admired each other's work.

In the summer of 1930 Evelyn travelled to Clarksville to see her mother for the first time in ten years. Maude Dunn had received no maintenance from her former husband and relied for sustenance and shelter on the grudging generosity of relatives and on the small sums which both Evelyn and Cyril sent from time to time. The relatives had begun to bitterly complain about the burden of keeping Mrs Dunn while her daughter toured Europe in style and had just written a novel which had made $100,000. They were unaware that the European travel was done on charity or borrowed cash, and that *The Wave* sold only 13,000 copies in eight years, excluding a very unlucrative book-club arrangement. *Escapade*, Evelyn's other 'big seller', sold 3,600 copies in five years and, when reissued by Cape and Smith in 1929, sold only 550 copies in four years.

The Clarksville relatives regarded Evelyn as a fallen woman, and it took some difficulty to persuade them that she could not take extra responsibility for her mother; this, and the strain of re-encountering the possessively affectionate Mrs Dunn, ensured that the visit was not a pleasant one.

From Clarksville she travelled up to New York to meet John, who was physically drained by the hardship of the voyage and the onset of illness. They decided to winter in England together, with no apparent motive except, perhaps, homesickness on John's part. The time in New Mexico was not over, but it was another year before Evelyn returned to the landscape she had so taken to heart.

20

An Interlude of Discovery

THE WINTER in England was uneventful. The couple stayed for several weeks in the house of John's aged aunt and sole surviving close relative, in Chislehurst. Aunt Mary was a frail old lady who would inevitably address Evelyn as E-ve-line, in memory of a sister who had died in childhood. She was also very rich, with no children to inherit her legacy, and John foresaw that her death would relieve him of poverty for ever.

From here they travelled to London to see publishers, then went down to Falmouth in Cornwall, where they took a winter let on a cottage. Evelyn recommenced work on *A Calendar of Sin* and announced to Lola that she had completed 367 pages of a new draft in nine weeks and that she had entirely scrapped the Santa Fé version. It was a period of nothing but work under the leaden skies of a Cornish winter, with each acting as nursemaid to the other, tending the colds which they seemed to catch alternately. In March they moved to Salisbury but things were no better there. 'Salisbury is the greyest place I have ever visited [...] I don't like England this year. It's too discouraging. I feel so sharply having been cut away from this two hundred years ago and left with the crude earth of such an unEnglish world. And can never go back,' she complained to Lola. Nor, according to Evelyn's assessment, did John feel at home. 'Jack's a dear but he isn't well and his country seems to make him too sadly its own. I don't think he's any happier over here.'

John's new book of macabre short stories, *Judas*, was ready for publication. This should have cheered him considerably, since they were a great advance on *The Smoking Leg* but, with the ill-luck both writers experienced with publishers, Constable was undergoing a change of ownership. The book was poorly advertised and sold a good deal less than it deserved.

Lola Ridge, meanwhile, was staying at Yaddo, in Saratoga Springs. She had written enthusiastically about her time there and had given the names of Evelyn and John as candidates for invitation. Their candidature was accepted and, with destitution once more looming dangerously near, they decided to take up the offer and sailed for America in June 1931.

Even in the greyness of Salisbury, Evelyn's uncanny talent for homing in on literary promise still functioned. Whilst browsing in a public library she came across a slim volume, almost a novella, and recognised a spark of greatness in its author. Sailing to America on the *Aquitania*, she wrote a letter of appreciation to the writer of the book via her publisher. The writer replied in turn, and another unlikely friendship began to develop.

The book which Evelyn picked up, *After Leaving Mr Mackenzie*, was the third publication by an author who called herself, in public and private life, Jean Rhys. Both her previous books had been published in America, had received, over-all, favourable reviews but had not sold. The same was true of her reception in England, and Evelyn's letter of praise was so welcome that Jean replied on the day she received it. 'I am always being told that until my work ceases being "sordid" and "depressing", I haven't much chance of selling,' she observed. The author of *The Narrow House* was too aware of such strictures herself, but she could not have known the many other ways in which their respective lives were paralleled.

Jean Rhys was born in Roseau, Dominica, in 1890 and christened Ella Gwendolyn Rees Williams. She left the island at the age of seventeen for schooling and dramatic training in England, a course she quickly abandoned for life as a chorus girl. From here onward, the facts of her life mix inextricably with her autobiographical fictions and it is difficult to separate the two strands. After experimentation with a number of pseudonyms, she finally adopted the name of Jean Rhys. As a chorus girl she had an affair with a rich older man which resulted in pregnancy and an abortion, after which she lived for a time on cheques from her former lover. Immediately after the First World War she married Jean Lenget, an adventurer whose sources of income remain imprecise and the couple lived a hand-to-mouth existence around Europe. In 1924 Lenget was imprisoned and, with a child to look after and absolutely penniless, she was rescued by Ford Madox Ford and there began the triangle fictionalised in her first novel, *Quartet*.

Ford was living with an Australian painter, Stella Bowen, who left an account of Jean which is unsympathetic, but almost certainly accurate:

The girl was a really tragic person. She had written an unpublishably sordid novel of great sensitiveness and persuasiveness, but her gift for prose and her personal attractiveness were not enough to ensure her any reasonable life, for on the other side of the balance were bad health, destitution, shattered nerves, an undesirable husband, lack of nationality, and a complete absence of any desire for independence. When we met her she possessed nothing but a cardboard suitcase and the astonishing manuscript. She was down to her last three francs and she was sick [...]

She took the lid off the world that she knew, and showed us an underworld of darkness and disorder, where officialdom, the bourgeoisie and the police were the eternal enemies and the fugitive the only hero. All the virtues, in her view, were summed up in 'being a sport', which meant being willing to take risks and show gallantry and share one's last crust; more attractive qualities, no doubt, than patience or honesty or fortitude. She regarded the law as the instrument of the 'haves' against the 'have nots' and was well acquainted with every rung of that long and dismal ladder by which the respectable citizen descends toward degradation.

Ford became her lover and literary mentor and she moved on the fringes of literary Bohemia, a world she was to depict in her first book of short stories, *The Left Bank*. Like Evelyn, she never became part of the Montparnasse establishment and her being there at all resulted from circumstance rather than literary ambition.

The affair with Ford ended as Jean Lenget was released from

prison, and his knowledge of it ended the marriage also. After a brief period with him in Amsterdam, Jean returned to England where she met Leslie Tilden-Smith, a literary agent who was to become her lover and later husband. In 1929 she began living with him, and in 1930 came the publication of *After Leaving Mr Mackenzie*.

Though the novel related to Jean's residence in Paris, it gave little indication of the similarities between the lives of Evelyn and Jean. Both were raised in Creole milieus but had found their way to England, a country both regarded with some antipathy. Both experienced great poverty, though Evelyn was more resourceful than Jean in obtaining money. And what may have attracted Evelyn to Jean's work was the sensibility portrayed, for both women held a deeply paranoid world-view. In her personal life, it was Jean's tragedy that she never encountered a Cyril; a rock who could be depended on for material and psychological aid when the current object of desire proved fallible. Leslie Tilden-Smith was chronically feckless with money and shared Jean's fondness for alcoholic excess. The men in her novels are often insubstantial figures who provide erratic material sustenance in return for sexual favours. As in Evelyn's books, the reader is given no clue as to why one man should be preferred to another; sex, when it occurs, just happens.

It is unsurprising that Evelyn should be among the few who recognised Jean's talent in the thirties. She did a great deal for *After Leaving Mr Mackenzie* in America, recommending the book in the New York *Herald-Tribune*, and privately to her friends. To Waldo Frank she characterised Jean as, 'one of the purest artists I have ever met with, though her canvases are limited'. She also recommended the book in an article on women novelists written for the *American Spectator*, with the observation that Jean Rhys 'has purified her work of vulgarising gentility'. She pertinently added that 'though this is pre-eminently a woman's story, the art of Jean Rhys makes it chaste to sexlessness'.

But this article was never printed and, in spite of a number of good notices, the book was a commercial failure in America. Jean began work on *Voyage in the Dark*, and periodically complained in her letters of the futility of producing work so little appreciated. Evelyn provided encouragement and continued to recommend her. 'She is always the writer I shall be proudest, if I can, to help find the public,' Evelyn wrote to Leslie Tilden-Smith.

The public for the novels of both women contracted through the thirties and *Voyage in the Dark* was a commercial failure like its predecessor. Neither Evelyn nor John mixed greatly in British literary circles and Evelyn's position in New York was weakened by her quarrelsomeness, her frequent absences and her political stridency. While in England the two couples met often and Jean, unlike some other of Evelyn's women friends, seems to have taken a liking to John. Jean's isolation from literary circles was almost complete, in spite of the fact that Leslie worked in publishing, and typically she had little interest in acquainting herself with her contemporaries:

I have not met other writers often. A few in Paris. Ford of course. Even fewer in England. That does not matter at all, for all the writer that matters is in the book or books. It is idiotic to be curious about the person. I have never made that mistake. Hey, what's all this about? Well, I say to myself, I have to feel my way. And damn badly you're doing it. Start again. It was Jack, who is a writer, who told me that my hatred for England was thwarted love. I said disappointed love maybe.

Outside the correspondence, this reference to Jack Metcalfe is the only allusion in Jean's published or unpublished writing to this friendship. The letters between the two women were detailed regarding their respective health problems, and contained a great deal of mutual praise. But Evelyn had little chance to offer concrete assistance to Jean until she and Leslie visited America in 1936. Two years earlier, Leslie had been left £8,000 by his father and, though much of this had been extravagantly spent, the residue financed a return to Dominica followed by several weeks in New York. Here Evelyn organised two parties to introduce Jean to her literary friends. The first, at a restaurant, seems to have been a success, but the second was a complete disaster. This took place at the apartment of Charles Studin, an elderly man unconnected formally with literature, who ran a sort of salon for aspiring and established talent. It is not certain who attended the party, but a number of people, Thomas Wolfe included, were invited because Jean admired their writing.

On the evening of the party Jean was feeling ill. She had been drinking a great deal that day and during the previous weeks. She somehow formed the impression that people at the party – Evelyn included – were hostile toward her. She made a terrible scene, for which she apologised profusely in her next two letters; letters which were to be the last she wrote to Evelyn. She felt that though she had probably overreacted there had been hostility toward her, and her contrition was qualified by that fact:

Except that – as regards persecution maniacs (this is one of my pet subjects) – Persecution maniacs (so called) always have been and usually still are, the victims of persecution. Of course they're called maniacs. It's part of the game Society plays – let's pretend that there's no such thing as this petty, leering, unsplendid cruelty, this damnable dropping of water on the same place for years, this mean bloody awful hatred of everything that isn't exactly like your mean self.

Whether the incident affected Jean's chance of acceptance by the New York literary world is open to question but, on balance, it does not seem likely that it did. It may have affected her relationship with Evelyn for shortly afterward the correspondence ceased. Both women, so unlike intellectually, had too much in common temperamentally to remain friends for long and in 1936 Evelyn was permanently resident in America and beset by personal crises of her own. She never found Jean her public though she continued to do what she could, and remained her main critical champion in America.

The rest of the Jean Rhys story has entered literary legend. In 1939 came publication of *Good Morning, Midnight*, in which the 'Jean Rhys woman', whose history was charted in the previous novels, reaches her nadir in the arms of a gigolo. Both she and her creator disappeared, until a radio dramatisation of *Good Morning, Midnight* set in motion a chain of events which led to the republication of the novels and her discovery by a new audience, and to the completion and publication of *Wide Sargasso Sea*. This novel explored Jean's childhood in Dominica through the eyes of Rochester's mad wife, prior to the events recounted in *Jane Eyre*. Jean's identification with the character is unmistakable and, though much of her difficult behaviour was ascribed to her drinking, it is clear that drink served only to conceal a deeper personality disorder.

Despite this, and a sensibility which made life burdensome, she survived forty years of poverty and neglect as a writer to find her own public. The almost supernatural spark of recognition between the two wholly dissimilar novelists led to nothing concrete, yet Jean Rhys became proof of a prediction Evelyn made to Emma Goldman in 1927, when she was struggling with a sense of futility: 'Print has a wonderful way of keeping alive an unexpectedly long time, and of emerging finally somehow from all efforts to extinguish it.'

After landing in New York and visiting Lola and other old friends, John and Evelyn travelled almost immediately up to Saratoga Springs. Yaddo, in 1931, maintained a lower profile than that institution currently does, and invitation was usually by publishers' or previous guests' recommendation. Its administrator, then and for many years to come, was a Minneapolis widow called Mrs Ames. Evelyn and Mrs Ames become fond of each other and Evelyn dedicated *Eva Gay* to her. Not all Yaddo guests enjoyed Mrs Ames' regime, which was strict on matters of house discipline though liberal on sexual behaviour and general high-spiritedness, but she dominated the institution until she was gently forced to resign by the directors when she was in her eighties. During her reign the routine never changed. Breakfast was served at eight in the beautiful dining room, or in bed, before the work period which ran from 9.00 a.m. to 4.00 p.m. During this time the writer was free from all distraction though, it was said, there was a gap in the hedge of the magnificent Italian gardens surrounding the house which gave on to the Saratoga Springs racecourse.

Horace Gregory was a fellow guest and his memoir *The House on Jefferson Street* recalls the tensions which grew between other visitors, most of whom were young, Depression-haunted and visibly bewildered by this sudden elevation to luxury: 'Some felt guilty at having their breakfasts served in bed, and tried to voice their complaints in Marxian rhetoric; others suggested that certain of their fellow guests be put on kitchen duty and made to mow the lawns of the estate.' Given Evelyn's aristocratic demeanour and absence of enthusiasm for class struggle, it is likely that she was recommended for kitchen duty and gardening, rather than her recommending others.

She spent three months at Yaddo, during which she finished a substantial part of her new novel, *Eva Gay*. She became very friendly with Horace and Marya Gregory and initially took to Oakley Johnson, a future luminary of literary communism whom she found 'very sensitive'. However, by the end of her stay her dubious tolerance of communists had turned into dislike and mistrust. The period had been productive and it was with some trepidation that she left the colony, at which board was free, to an uncertain financial future which depended on good sales of *A Calendar of Sin*. John had decided to return to England again so, in late October 1931, after seeing John off, she decided to return West to see her first family.

21

Way Out West - 2

EVELYN FOUND that she stepped straight into a hornets' nest on her return. Cyril had given up running the art school he had founded after being offered the post of director of the newly formed Denver Art Museum and the move had aggravated various petty jealousies against him in the Santa Fé art colony. At Denver one of his first acts was to arrange an exhibition of forty watercolours bequeathed to him by Owen Merton, who died of a brain tumour in a London hospital in January 1931. The rapid collapse of Cyril's marriage and the subsequent divorce from Phyllis Crawford began a flurry of rumour which gained fresh momentum when Evelyn returned unaccompanied by John Metcalfe. There was strong speculation, completely unfounded, that Evelyn had conspired toward the break-up.

During her previous stay in Santa Fé, Evelyn had befriended and become emotionally involved with a writer called Don Clark, and a counter-rumour held that she had left John to become his mistress. Don Clark who, under the name of Axton Clark, published an undistinguished volume of verse called *The Single Glow*, was a plump art historian whose impulses were basically homosexual; a condition which Evelyn took great pains to deny. Their relationship resumed and continued to a point of deterioration at which he fled to California and announced that he would not return until Evelyn had left. As a Santa Féan who viewed the town's hermetic social world from the inside, he resented her criticisms of the colony's activities. As they were voiced in a letter to Lola: 'Oh to have some real escape into this country whose vastness at present seems to exist only to emphasise the picayune nature of humans. I look at the very mountains as if they had betrayed me by being gorgeous and aloof [...] As your middle-class English, so these arty Americans, who cannot take it seriously that there is any preoccupation more satisfying than theirs with their sneaking little sexualities that have to be bootleg-ged like the liquor and then boasted about.'

Evelyn had returned to be with Creighton, whom she had not seen for over a year. But there were problems here too. At the age of sixteen, Creighton had secretly married his father's 23-year-old secretary in June 1931. The event had been much gossiped about but had not yet been made officially public and Cyril, who was suffering from a weak heart, had yet to be told. As well as being director of the Denver Art Museum, he was also Dean of the College of Fine Arts at the University of Denver and his son's unorthodox marriage would impress neither his students' parents nor his sponsors. The Carnegie Institute had given ten thousand dollars to the school and there was a distinct possibility that, having once more found a good foothold, it would be knocked from under him by scandal. But, as usual, he weathered the storm successfully.

Evelyn was destitute again and applied for a Guggenheim award for which she felt she had little chance. She continued work on *Eva Gay*, a novel 'more personal than anything I did since *Escapade*'. With some simplifications it was a *roman à clef* which traced her early life and her involvements with Cyril and Owen Merton. Though its content diverged from truth, it can be assumed that her perception of the two characters in the novel reflected her attitude toward their real-life counterparts. Cyril is the austere biologist Hans Haaska, for whom Evelyn has a love closer to agape than eros, and whose responsibility toward Eva verges on the paternal. Merton is Evan Garrett, an unstable, half-crazed caricature of a starving artist to whom Eva is drawn in a complex part-sexual, part-maternal way. Relations between the two men are those of hostile envy and admiration by Garrett for Haaska and a condescending contempt by Haaska for Garrett. Garrett eventually dies of a brain tumour and the novel ends in New York with Haaska reflecting on the limits of individualism as a course of action. Evelyn described the book as 'pure anarchist' to Lola; the closing pages include a scene in which Haaska discusses Marxist attitudes with a group of very wooden Soviet apologists:

'Well, individualism's done for, anyhow, thank Pete!' young Murray Pearce declared. 'It went out with the philosophical anarchists of the last century. The whole damn movement went into an orgy about sex. All they were after was a chance to sleep with any one they wanted to. That's one step to emancipation, I admit; but it's not important.'

'Yes,' Felix Baudenburg said solemnly, 'we can't be taken in by that subjective stuff again. It works right in with the religious myth; and no one has to bust his bean to see what *that* has done! In the future society, thank god, we won't have any parasites to get a hold on people through that phony bunk. The only brain workers we will allow will be the scientists. They are some good.'

Not unnaturally, Haaska compares such attitudes to the Puritans, whom he finds to be slightly preferable. The novel rejects not only communist ideas, but also the tenets on which Evelyn's early life had been based. Five years later she was to write that the book 'described the failure in fact of an application of an anarchistic philosophy to the solution of emotional needs of strongly individualised temperaments'. In a deep sense, the novel rejected her own past.

She was no longer an anarchist and would describe herself for most of the thirties as a 'liberal'. *Eva Gay* was the first of three novels dealing with the artist and the problem of creativity in a commercial world. Evelyn's 'liberalism' rarely concerned itself with matters outside the narrow realm of aesthetics and she was, by and large, silent on the rise of the dictators, Spain, mass unemployment and the other paramount questions of the thirties. Even the correspondence with Emma Goldman lacks political comment on specific issues, though there is much theoretical discussion. As she would observe in 1937, her admiration was reserved for the rebel:

That the logic of Marxism, in its present extension to cover things Marx never treated of in detail, was far from clear to me when I regarded myself as three-quarters Marxist, I now realise, for I remember how my sympathies went out to a series of Anarchist philosophers, also, without ever making me feel a line was to be drawn and an exclusive allegiance declared. Rebellion had developed in my own character, and I loved a rebel. I loved best men whose rebellion constituted a championing of the socially abused.

The individualism of the thirties novels encumbered them with a weight of anti-ideological baggage. Second only to communists in the firing line were art entrepreneurs: publishers and picture dealers, whom she depicted in a rather Marxian way as the natural foe of the artist. Unlike Jean Rhys she could not ignore political questions nor was she able to erect an evolved liberal philosophy as an alternative to communism, as Kay Boyle did. She had little faith in the present efficacy of Emma Goldman's ideas; it was the woman she admired.

The class of artists and rebels is a numerically small one, and in the fraught political atmosphere of the thirties her voice was easily drowned. The cause of individualism in that decade was the least popular flag under which to march.

Santa Fé was turning sour and Evelyn felt increasingly that she was becoming a staple of local gossip; a sense which threw her back mentally to the most unpleasant years of her life, when her family, impoverished and held together by convention only, was lodging with her conspicuously deranged grandmother in New Orleans. Furthermore, she found she no longer enjoyed the kind of artistic enclave into which she had plunged with such enthusiasm ten years earlier in the Village. Personal relationships were becoming increasingly difficult and, in March 1932, she left the West, never to return. After a brief spell visiting friends in New York, she sailed over to England to rejoin her husband once more.

22

Speaking of Herself

EVELYN BEGAN her career as a mysterious exile in Brazil and for much of the twenties was spiritually and physically distant from the American cultural mainstream. The re-establishment of her career with *The Wave* and the fact that during the thirties she divided her time between England and America and ceased her distant wanderings meant that, as far as the world of books was concerned, she became a more accessible figure. She began to write criticism and book reviews again, contributed a number of short stories to magazines and also was the subject of several feature articles on writers.

When the quintessential organ of twenties revolt, the *Little Review*, ceased publication in 1929, the last issue was devoted to a questionnaire addressed to various past and present contributors on their personal and aesthetic stances. Evelyn had not been a contributor except for the debate on the art of madness, but she was sent a questionnaire and submitted answers of such length that they had to be cut. Her responses were couched in the verbose language beloved of the *Little Review*, but they are, none the less, highly illuminating.

Evelyn claimed to want no knowledge except self-realisation, and wanted to be no more than she was. She had no wish to change places with another human being – indeed, the idea was alien to her. 'There is no getting rid of the constancy of the first person singular – even by giving it a plural description.' She looked forward to death as a release, or to an old age without stress. She feared poverty, more suffering of those she loved, their death before hers and, ominously, 'perhaps the fear of insanity is as great'.

Happiness came not through experience but from the cessation of worry and the ending of pain after discomfort. She listed her weaknesses as: the equivalent of the absence of a sense of humour, a deficiency of *savoir faire*, thin-skinnedness, fear worship, a perpetual anticipation of the worst, a fatuous trust in 'human nature', a physical inferiority complex, an instinct against concealment, an intense pain capacity and moral pride.

On the credit side she claimed moral courage and an undivertable mentality, emotional directness, illimitable curiosity, an intense capacity for pleasure, an imagination which could identify with any person to whose existence she had even a fragmentary key, and a definition of equality as being more than equality of advantage. She thought that the latter was her best attribute.

She felt that the most hopeful symptom of contemporary art was the recovery of the romantic impulse from the cheapness of its cliché associations. Freud, Expressionism and, inexplicably, Einstein, were landmarks of this path. She continued to live because she was not in a state of insupportable discontent.

The questionnaire, with its stress on subjective probing, reflected an attitude toward the creative process which was already becoming outmoded as the questions were voiced. Shadowing almost all of Evelyn's published writings and the whole intellectual atmosphere of the twenties was the figure of Freud. Her letters are dotted with phrases such as 'Freudianly explicable', and 'Freudianly understandable'. She sent Creighton to several analysts and consulted them herself from 1928 on, when funds allowed. Creighton's second wife, Paula, who grew up in the Taos colony, remembered that her childhood was coloured by Freud to a degree which now seems unimaginable.

The star of Freud as guiding light to the intelligentsia was already waning as American capitalism, after half a century of untrammelled expansion, hit its first major obstacle. The theoretical end of analysis was personal freedom, the same goal the twenties radicals aimed for. The height of artistic expression was the pure unimpeded voice of the artist. In the twenties the artist finally absolved himself of responsibility to an audience and it was in that decade that he reached new distances of splendid isolation from the public. This was the modern movement.

To the emergent thinkers of the thirties the duty of the artist was not self-transformation but the transformation of society as a whole. It was decreed by them that freedom in isolation was an illusion unless linked with the working-class movement; future questionnaires would canvass opinion on specific world issues rather than indulge in psychological probing. The pendulum swinging between the poles of individualism and collectivism was about to swing back decisively.

Evelyn was twice the subject of features in the *American Bookman*. In the October 1929 issue a critical article by Robert Morss Lovett averred that her purpose was 'purely aesthetic'. He felt that pain was predominant in her work and experience and saw *Escapade* as the key to the unremitting distaste for life exhibited in the early books. The broadening of perspective in *The Wave* was the fruition of her previous prose experiments.

On her first visit to Yaddo in 1931, Evelyn struck up a friendship with a writer called Harry Salpeter. She evidently charmed him, as his feature for the *American Bookman* of November 1931 indicates: 'So this was she. A small slight restless bodied woman dressed in a black evening gown that turned to lace at throat and sleeves [...] Even in repose she suggests energies held in nervous reserve.'

He also observed there were times when she conveyed the impression that she was born to be the châtelaine of an estate, apparently unaware that, in terms of the American South, she had been. Evelyn told him that *The Narrow House* had been the most intense book she had written, but pointed out that it was fragmentary and lacked the philosophical content which a major novel should have. She described her method of writing as the initial composition of a rough draft, of equal length to the finished work, which was then worked into a final draft. And she stated her aim as a writer:

I want to make my own universe recognisable to others; I want to communicate my sense of what life is to me. I don't expect anyone to know what my universe is until I'm dead and it has been completed. One book can be only a partial attempt to create, or express, the universe. There is something in each one of my books that makes it an integral part of the architecture of the whole and even if, at my death, a turret should be missing, you will still be able to get an idea of the general design – at least I hope so.

Theodore Dreiser wrote to Evelyn in 1932 asking for a contribution to the *Spectator*, which was then being floated. At the time Dreiser was engaged in one of his periodic flirtations with the Communist Party and Evelyn wondered in her reply whether she would be radically orthodox enough. Dreiser reassured her that there would be no problem.

However, she was too unorthodox for the *Spectator*. She submitted two articles, 'Religion versus Religion' and 'The Decline of Feminism and the Metamorphosis of the Feminist' and both were spiked. Eventually two articles contrasting England and America, 'Voyager's Return' and 'Gentlemanly Englishmen – and Americans', were accepted and printed.

On submitting her piece on feminism, she told Dreiser that she was 'one of the few still in captivity, so it ought to be interesting, like psychic communication with an extinct pterodactyl'. The article was pessimistic, rose to an anti-Soviet climax and a most unhopeful close. She felt she had witnessed the growth and decline of old-fashioned feminism. Art as a door to women's self-expression had been locked by the Church and by republican governments. The rise of the machine had granted economic independence only to a few. A true feminism would investigate women's slavery in nature rather than in society, by which she meant, largely, her biologically ordained maternal role. She felt that agitation for birth control was the only effort currently being made to raise the dignity of woman and liberate her personality. Though the Soviet Union had apparently enlightened attitudes toward contraception and maternity, she saw nothing in Marxism, a philosophy which presumed that biological standards defined progress, to suggest that this policy might not be reversed at any instant. In all the achievement of feminism had been small and on the future status of women, 'to imagine her as passing from this just perceptible dawn into another darkness does not seem to me fantastic'.

The freedom which interested her was an existential liberation rather than one attainable by social reform; questions of suffrage and equality of wages, education and opportunity were not even raised. Like Emma Goldman she placed great emphasis on the need for birth control. 'The affront to personal dignity which must follow when the one sanctioned role for a woman is that of a medium for unelected propagation' was, to her, the core of the feminist dilemma.

Evelyn's feminism had more in common with resurgent contemporary feminism than with the reformists who then constituted the mainstream of feminist thought. These were to be absorbed, more or less, wholesale, into the communist movement and feminism as a major current of thought would die with that movement. However, it would be too much to see the essay as a prophecy of new feminism, or to see Evelyn Scott as a proto-feminist of the contemporary mould. She was silent on most issues which concern modern feminists and in her private life showed a dependence on a male partner which many would find appalling. Her individualism was not conducive to group awareness, nor did it allow for concerted action and, as so often, the uniqueness of her ideas placed her beyond simple categorisation.

Evelyn spent much of her life in England with an English husband and wrote a novel with an English setting. The country which was her second home generated fascination and repulsion as, however, did her native land. Like many Americans her perception of English society was conditioned by its peculiarities of class structure. Though reared under what she termed 'the tin-pot feudalism of the post-Civil War South', the nuances of caste separating one Briton from another were as alien to her as those operative in Delhi. The Englishman was a gentleman or nothing, she proclaimed, and his gentlemanliness proclaimed itself through a self-effacement which she contrasted unfavourably with the overt individualism of America. He was, as myth held him to be, cold, and 'on the theme of himself and his affections, a mystic'. She felt that aristocratic values had percolated through society and held even the working class in thrall. And she had met, and been irritated by, the young Oxford Marxists whom she compared with the nobles of the French Revolution who read Rousseau and dug their own graves.

Most of her observations were commonplaces, though pithily expressed, and it is interesting to speculate how much they owed to that reticent, self-effacing man, John Metcalfe. In 1932 Metcalfe spent a good deal of his limited funds in joining the Savile Club and he maintained his subscriptions lifelong, even when exiled for many years in America. He seems to have been a model of English conservatism and one wonders what he made of Emma Goldman and the Bohemian sets he encountered in New York and the South-West. His influence may have been responsible for a growing conservatism in Evelyn's behaviour, though other former rebels were also straightening out. Writing to Lola in 1932, Evelyn mentioned that the Theis couple were now very anti-Bohemian and oriented toward success.

Many of those who quit America in the twenties for Paris had returned home. The Europe they left was already shadowed by the rise of the dictators and, in contrast, even the commercial vulgarities of America seemed symptoms of health. Soon they would polarise between those who felt that capitalism was doomed and those who felt that, with a few adjustments, the American way could be preserved. The paper war of the thirties was about to begin in earnest.

23

A Rough Passage

AFTER A ROUGH crossing on the *Mauretania*, Evelyn arrived in England to find John in poor health and low in spirits. She also learned that her American publishers, Jonathan Cape and Harrison Smith, had gone bankrupt, robbing her of any money she might have made on *A Calendar of Sin*. She was financially saved only by receipt of a Guggenheim award, and her suspicion of publishers' wiles was reinforced. She complained to Emma Goldman:

> I don't know where I'd be without it [the Guggenheim award], as there was no way of disentangling my Calendar contract from Cape after Hal [Harrison Smith] left there, and now Cape is bankrupt and I shall get twenty five cents on the dollar *sometime* – god knows when. Also I received a statement from Cape in April, before the bankruptcy, and it reported exactly one fifth the number of sales now reported to me by the auditor sent in from outside to make out statements for the bankruptcy creditors. Bloody old crook! Cape, I mean. What a gang.

Harrison Smith set up a new firm with Robert Haas which was to publish *Eva Gay* and the subsequent novel, *Breathe Upon These Slain*. Hal Smith was one of the few friends Evelyn retained in the publishing world, though even he had offended her on the last night before departure for England, by trying to persuade her to let him publish *Eva Gay* without an advance. Evelyn worked on the book in the suburbs of South London through the summer of

1932, one of the wettest for many years. By September *Eva Gay* was finished, and she began work immediately on a children's novel, *Billy the Maverick*, eventually published in 1934. John was at work on what was to be, in the opinion of some critics, his best novel. Based in part on his childhood experiences in Dr Barnardo's homes, *Foster Girl* explored the seedy, sinister, lower-middle-class milieu which he had established as his fictional territory in the earlier novels.

Though working consistently, Evelyn found time for correspondence with Waldo Frank on his panegyric to the Revolution, *Dawn in Russia*. The book exhibited a revolutionary masochism which she found repellent; Frank seemed to hint that he would understand fully if the dynamic of the Revolution required that he be liquidated. Their friendship was strong enough to survive these attitudes and, besides, their current phases of writing had much in common. Frank himself was engaged in a semi-autobiographical book, *The Death and Birth of David Markand*, which, like *Eva Gay*, was in part a recanting of previously held attitudes.

In autumn came the news, greeted with relief by Evelyn, that Creighton's ill-considered marriage was over. The couple had been living in New York and Creighton had returned West to Denver and his father, leaving his wife behind.

In October Evelyn and John moved to Lowestoft, a quiet, unfashionable fishing town on the East Anglian coast. Evelyn's letters on the English were more forthright than she was in her *Spectator* article. To Lola:

We were mad with depression in London. The English are cold, Lola. I was thinking recently that never once has any English person made a gesture of real friendship toward me or an imaginative one to ease the foreignness. Sensitive and cold together. Cold in utter indifference to the fate of everything not touching them immediately, just in theory, and sensitive and mystical regarding what is at the inner core of their lives. They are, therefore, satisfactory in a love relation, but in friendship only after a long, long time and when special occasions break the ice.

The coldness she detected in the people was matched meteorologically as a wet summer gave way to a freezing winter.

Occasionally they visited London to see friends of John or to call
on Jean Rhys, and on one of these visits they met Geoffrey
Grigson, then about to found *New Verse*, one of the most important poetry magazines of the thirties. He was looking for contributors and Evelyn suggested Lola Ridge. Writing to David
Lawson, Lola's husband, in January 1933 she queried: 'Geoffrey
Grigson, an English youth, is starting a poetry mag. and said he
would write and ask Lola for something. I wonder if he ever did?'
    In 1981 Grigson recalled the impecunious couple who were to
remain his friends for a number of years:

Yes, I knew Evelyn Scott and John Metcalfe fairly well a
thousand years ago. She was a darling, and would be wrongly
described as 'bohemian', which word wouldn't please her.
Metcalfe was vaguely sinister (a word which wouldn't please
him either) – see his book of short stories *The Smoking Leg*,
perhaps unfairly forgotten (many short stories appeared in the
London 'Evening Standard'). Very well, they were (as a rule)
penniless, and in London they used to stay at a very extraordinary ex-convicts' hotel off Theobalds Road. Theobalds
Road in the thirties was a squalid tumbledown area. I forget the
name, but the sheets, pillow cases, towels, etc. were all marked
Theobalds Hotel: Stolen Property – if that was, after all, the
name. Then John came into some £20,000 or maybe less, from
an aunt I think, and the two of them blew the whole of it in a few
months of high life.
    I'm afraid I remember little else about Evelyn except her
looks – very appealing – and her manner, very generous and
warm. Her (chief?) novel was a flop in England, I think. I do
remember a story Evelyn told about a generous whore in New
York who was closeted in a public loo when she heard a
scraping and a wheezing from the next compartment; and over
the division there appeared the head of a tramp. The whore
slipped out of her compartment, slipped into the tramp's and
gave him – free of course – out of the kindness of her heart
exactly what he wanted, a piece of woman. Evelyn described it
as the most generous act she had ever come across.

Is this the 'desperately intellectual' neurotic Kay Boyle met in a
Paris café nine years earlier, or the intense poseur Robert

McAlmon had seen through in the Theis apartment? The testimony of those who met Evelyn merely adds to the contradictions already apparent in her life. The legacy which Grigson remembers was certainly less than £20,000. It was blown but, as will emerge, on things a good deal less enjoyable than high life.

The couple shivered through a winter at Lowestoft, again nursing each other through a succession of colds. They planned to return to America in April, when John had to be there to renew his quota entry status, but publication of *Eva Gay* was held up so they stayed in England living on the dwindling remnant of the Guggenheim money. The return fare would be paid by the advance Evelyn was to receive on the novel. She described the year as her worst since 1925, and felt desperate with worry about the future. The clouds parted for a while when they learned that they had been invited back to Yaddo and, as if in unconscious preparation, Evelyn added *Das Kapital* to the list of books she was reading. It was in depressed spirits and with little security that the couple took a third-class tourist passage on the *Bremen* for another attempt at life together in America.

Evelyn returned just in time for the publication of *Eva Gay* to mixed but generally approving reviews. One perceptive dissenter was Jonathan Daniels in the *Saturday Review of Literature*, who remarked that her books were 'monuments of literary megalomania', and went on to suggest that she was really a Gothic novelist in the tradition of Ann Radcliffe. 'One feels that Miss Scott has made her sexual complexities and sexual fears in much the same spirit that Mrs Radcliffe devised her more frankly romantic horrors and mysteries [...] The truth is that Miss Scott merely frightens with the phallus as Mrs Radcliffe did with ghosts. The fashion, not the method, has changed.' The book had the recommendation of the Book of the Month Club, and sold reasonably well.

Among its readers was Frederick Wellman, a son by Cyril's first marriage. Cyril felt that his depiction as Hans Haaska was 'unrecognisable'; none the less, it was sufficiently accurate for his long-estranged son to realise that the author of the book must have known his father. Frederick Wellman contacted Cyril's other three children by the same marriage and urged them to read the book. They did so and agreed with Frederick Wellman.

Together they wrote to Evelyn, care of her publisher, and secured Cyril's address. He had lost contact with his first family who, he had been led to believe, had been turned against him by his staunchly Puritan first wife and her relatives. This had not been the case and there was a highly emotional family reunion in Wichita, Kansas, where two of his sons worked in journalism. Through this coincidence Cyril rediscovered his first family and learned that he now had grandchildren. He became increasingly close to the Wellmans in later years, eventually readopting his original name.

He was now an eminent figure in Denver and might have remained so were it not for the strain of the altitude on his weak heart. In 1934 he organised a retrospective of one hundred of the best paintings from his decade-long career as an artist, then announced his retirement from the Denver posts on health grounds. The last of his varied careers was over and, though he continued to paint and pursued an active retirement, this protean man would not embark on any new venture except the writing of his autobiography.

At Yaddo Evelyn and John, the latter enfeebled by what had now been diagnosed as amoebic dysentery, settled in for what was to be a long stay. As communicated to Lola, her first impressions of her fellow guests were favourable:

Mildly pleasant crowd here: Philip and Penina Reisman, painters, rather sweet enfants terribles. Ruth Suckow and her husband. A plaintive sycophant with a resourceful wit and a bruised self-respect named Charles Yale Harrison. A tall sea-going boy, intriguingly shy and to himself who writes Conradish stories, Floyd or Lloyd Collins. Grace Lumpkin, an elderly little girl, straightforward to bluntness and rather engaging. Albert Halper, who is so completely an average American that he's rather wonderful: as if at last one had actually met – what! A real cowboy, after the movies. Or a real Englishman. Or, or. But he's naively frank and all his mentality covers he regards from his own for him authentic angle. Carl Carmer, who is kinder and more sensitively aware of social obligations than anyone else, with qualifications as an artist that remain ambiguous. Louis Adamic, lusting for revenge on capital [...]

So she wrote the roseate bloom of first impressions. Things were to sour after her discovery that nearly all those present were fanatical communists and that lunchtime conversations tended to revolve monotonously around the theme of the coming American Revolution. The Reismans were young and had the fanaticism which, Evelyn recognised, she had once possessed when younger. Her suspicion of communist intentions was not lessened when Philip Reisman informed her that after the Revolution she would be one of the first to be shot. None the less, with the breadth of mind she felt she had attained on passing her fortieth birthday, she wrote to Harry Salpeter that she liked them. 'It is one of life's so frequent ironies to have to be, for one's own integrity, unsympathetic to a way of behaviour which was once one's own and very dear.'

Albert Halper, later author of *Union Square*, a memoir of thirties radicalism, and Louis Adamic, a Yugoslav immigrant who, in 1931, had published a book called *Dynamite. The Story of Class Violence in America*, were both Marxists. Adamic, however, was genial enough to retain Evelyn's friendship for some years to come. He was later assassinated for his beliefs, as was Evelyn's anarchist friend, Carlo Tresca, when the thirties paper war escalated to overt violence. Adamic reported that on one occasion Evelyn exclaimed, 'If I hear the word "revolution" once more at this table, I shall leave the dining room.' One of the radicals rose to the challenge and promptly hissed, 'Revolution! Revolution!' at which point Evelyn, true to her word, stalked out.

Such trivial incidents might have been brushed off by a person less sensitive or less prone to a paranoiac interpretation of events. For Evelyn, they confirmed her worst fears and her strident anti-communism dates from this second stay at Yaddo. At the end of the summer of 1933, she wrote to Lola that the atmosphere had been so uncongenial that little work had been done. She believed that her mail was being opened and read and that others regarded her as some sort of spy. For the winter she and John moved to a nearby farmhouse which was part of the estate and here Evelyn began serious work on *Breathe Upon These Slain*, a novel tracing the decline of an upper-middle-class English family. It was socially pessimistic, and again featured some grimly caricatured communists, waiting to pick up the shards of the old order. Apart from *Escapade*, it was her only venture into first-person writing and, though it was favourably received by critics on publication in 1934, it sold badly. In 1937 she wrote, 'In *Breathe Upon These Slain*, I tried to demonstrate the operation of a fictional imagination in a way to point philosophical implications in the creative process itself.' At heart it was a novel about the writing of novels and its vitality suffered as a result. When it was published in England the anonymous *Times Literary Supplement* reviewer remarked, 'Much care and thought and fine intelligence have clearly gone into the writing of this novel, but it lacks an artistic (as opposed to an intellectual) coherence and, at the heart of it, the real spark of life.'

Both Evelyn and John had bouts of illness but, by the spring of 1934, most of the book was completed. Other projects had taken up time, including canvassing support for Emma Goldman's readmission to America. At Waldo Frank's suggestion, and after a great deal of confusion, she had also written a piece for a seventieth-birthday tribute to Alfred Stieglitz. When the time came to leave Yaddo, John returned to England to seek medical treatment for his amoebic dysentery. Evelyn remained in America, putting the finishing touches to her novel and arranging publication, planning to follow on when this was done. The separation was meant to be brief but, as circumstance dictated, they were not reunited for over a year.

In June 1934, John wrote that treatment at the London School of Tropical Medicine was improving his condition and that he was consulting a Harley Street specialist. Payment for this came from the legacy of his aunt Mary, who had recently died and of whose estate he was trustee. The bulk of the inheritance went to an aunt-in-law and John received a lump sum rather than the life income he had hoped to inherit. With the residue left after his considerable medical bills had been paid, he bought a cottage in the village of Walberswick in Suffolk. His letters to Evelyn kept up a cheerful front, but the months of solitude did not improve his deteriorating mental condition. None the less he was in England, where he felt that he belonged, and a plan to visit America toward the end of 1934 was quietly dropped.

After publication of *Breathe Upon These Slain*, Evelyn quarrelled with Harrison Smith, who demanded $2,500 to release her from the contract with his firm. With or without payment, he eventually did so. She was now without a publisher and planning her magnum opus, a story of the French Revolution entitled *Before Cock Crow*. This was eventually contracted to Scribner through the legendary Max Perkins, who was John's American editor. Several advances were paid but the novel, which went through endless revisions, was never completed. Even in her most extreme denunciations of publishers, Evelyn never recanted her good opinion of Max Perkins.

The French Revolution novel required a great deal of research and, finding herself in the interim with no specific plan, she picked up the 1923 manuscript of the unpublished novel *The Grey Riddle*. This had undergone minor alterations through the years and she now subjected it to complete re-writing. As *Bread and a Sword* it was to be her first novel for Scribner in 1937. She also wrote a number of artistically unsuccessful short stories, several of which appeared in magazines and anthologies but none of which deserves especial comment. The form evidently did not suit her.

Her essay, 'A Note on the Esthetic Significance of Photography', appeared in the 1934 birthday tribute volume, *America and Alfred Stieglitz*. Most of the essay was an attack on Marxist aesthetics; photography, and Stieglitz himself, are granted token mention only in the last few paragraphs. Stieglitz, who once remarked, 'I am attracted by life, not doctrine. All isms contain a grain of truth', was not an ideologue; neither were most of the contributors. Anti-communism was now Evelyn's obsession and any soapbox, it seems, would do. Having been a lifelong radical of an indefinable sort, Evelyn felt betrayed by the wholesale turn of the progressive intelligentsia toward communism. As the failure of her lecture tour demonstrated, Emma Goldman, the political figure with whom Evelyn most identified, was yesterday's woman.

The real conservatives of American literature had long opted for exile in countries which had the ordered social structure they admired. A few remained. e.e.cummings combined his highly experimental verse with an intense political conservatism that had no room for even the Keynesian tinkerings of Roosevelt. In 1939 one of his young acolytes was a Yale scholar and admirer of Ezra Pound called James Jesus Angleton. Angleton did not follow up his early literary enthusiasms; instead, as head of the

CIA Counterintelligence Division, he became the vigilant foe of communism wherever he believed it might have raised its head.

Others opted for neutrality. William Carlos Williams remained apolitical except for a brief involvement with Social Credit while under Pound's influence. Most writers had vague left-wing sympathies, but kept these apart from the machinations of the Communist Party. The Red Thirties were largely a myth and even then, as Granville Hicks observed, it was always easier to be an anti-communist than a communist.

Evelyn was by nature a radical and a rebel and in making her criticisms from such a perspective she incurred more hostility than had she been simply conservative. Unlike Waldo Frank and Edmund Wilson, who thought communism might be 'personal-ised', she had no illusion that the Party machine was capable of reform. What irritated her was that the Party had hegemonised radical thought in her natural constituency of literary New York: the fact that its rhetoric scarcely reverberated beyond the dis-course of the intelligentsia was of small comfort. She was a writer who had never worked at any other trade and the New York literary world was, throughout all her wanderings, the milieu to which she would always return. Here, historic inevitability had made deep inroads; even the once staunch anarchist Lola Ridge drew a line between the moral ends of communism and the unpleasantness of some of its adherents. In her radical perspec-tive Evelyn was, as so often, alone on a limb.

During the thirties she devoted much effort to the Sisyphean task of destroying the intellectual foundations of Marxism; to little effect, since the results were never published. In two lengthy pieces, 'The Destruction of the Liberal' and 'The Fallacy of Marxist Doctrine', she alleged that her own liberal position was anomalous in the Marxist world-view. The purpose of art was antithetical to the purpose of the State and proletarian warfare was inimicable to the artist, the speculative scientist and the philosopher. 'The Fallacy of Marxist Doctrine' concluded, 'If [. . .] Marxism is able to dominate our social scene, it will bring the destruction of all superior minds.'

These criticisms went almost unheard except, when granted a public platform in a magazine or radio broadcast, she reiterated them to the point of tedium. Refutation of Marxism required either a single negative utterance, which she was temperamentally unable to make, or a lengthy, philosophically coherent study, which she was intellectually unequipped to make. Unlike Emma Goldman she had no programme, barring the highly relative standards of 'liberalism', with which to oppose the monolith. In the long run this would drive her into an increasingly conservative stance, along with many other former libertarians.

Her energetic career had reached a hiatus when, after fifteen months occupied mostly by reviewing, short story writing and feature writing, she rejoined John in England. By now, neither had the illusion that they could live happily in each other's native land but, since John had sunk his legacy into the Suffolk cottage, it seemed time for her to try once more to cultivate English roots.

The separation had been grim for John, much of it taken up with illness and medical treatment. On January 3, 1935 he had written a brief note to Jean Rhys, asking her to get in touch. He had been poorly, and then had a nurse in attendance, but worst of all was his depression. 'Do please write or something. I feel very very low, and I've so few friends anywhere,' the letter ended.

Walberswick was drenched with rain and Evelyn found John in poor physical and mental shape when she arrived. She felt immediate pangs of homesickness and, though she liked the cottage and situation, the feeling soon grew that the arrangement was not likely to last. 'If you really want to know how *not* to be contented: Remarry foreigners you each like as much as you like each other, and try, without an income, to live on both sides of the Atlantic at once!' Evelyn wrote to Lewis Gannett.

Much of their inevitably restricted social life they spent at the local Bell Hotel, which was run by a man who it was said had once been Galsworthy's valet. He was not the only connection with the literary world in the locality, for nearby lived A. E. Coppard, the short story writer published originally by *The Dial* in America. Coppard was a communist of working-class origins and in 1935 was in a particularly anti-American frame of mind. He and Evelyn argued on the subject of America on first meeting and, after she left Walberswick, they maintained a long argument by letter centred almost exclusively on communism.

Evelyn continued to work on *Bread and a Sword* and also gave much time and energy to her projected French Revolution novel. John had struggled through his several physical and mental complaints to complete *Foster Girl*, though Evelyn believed that his condition was serious enough to warrant analysis. Only a few months had elapsed before the couple began to talk about renting out the cottage and moving away. Evelyn was the prime mover behind this idea and her years of exile seem to have at last reconciled her to America. To Lola:

> I'm too, too American after all to really ever want a home forever here – maybe I wouldn't have in France though I used to think so. The aesthetic appeal in the older nations seemed to extend so much then, but when one lives through a number of highly personalised trials one wants the comfort of familiarity. Besides the Americans who grow into completely successful English are a bit Judas-like, always in the forefront to applaud all the misconceived criticism of USA – like the German-Americans in the war, the most English of all. Poor Jack – I wonder if he feels the same in US, and do we demand equally of the foreigner that he 'spit in his own face'? Or is that Ellis Island behaviour not current elsewhere?

Her nostalgia took a positive form when she signed a contract with Robert McBride, a New York publisher, for a short book on Tennessee. She postponed a planned visit to France and agreed to be in America by March 1, 1936, to do preliminary research. The atmosphere in England was clouded by Mussolini's invasion of Abyssinia, and there was a good deal of war-talk in the air. John was still an RAF reservist and he was warned to be prepared for action; action for which neither he nor Evelyn had much enthusiasm.

Finances were low as usual and the couple spent Christmas Day of 1935 with the Coppards, who were equally impoverished and also had two children to support. Fortunately a friend sent Evelyn $400 and on this, and the advance from McBride, she returned to America in February 1936, leaving John at Walberswick. Plans to rent out the cottage floundered, as John was still too ill to move, and it was eventually sold at a considerable loss.

24

Home - I

~~~~~~

ON ARRIVAL in New York, Evelyn rejoined Cyril and Creighton, who were now living on the East coast. Almost immediately she fell ill, and her visit to Clarksville had to be postponed. Instead she worked on *Bread and a Sword* and attempted to readjust to American life. First impressions of New York were not encouraging after rural Suffolk. 'I don't like New York again,' she wrote to Lola. 'I mean the tastelessness of the people, the complete absence of any integrity, the casual view of brutality have me down again. But I shall have my nerves rubbed down and like it once more with time I'm sure.'

The finished version of *Bread and a Sword* was to be far different from the proto-version composed fifteen years earlier. Its unusual style and method of narration made it Evelyn's most radically innovative novel and her closest approach to pure expressionism. It was a story of economic necessity versus artistic integrity, a theme close to her heart and to her personal circumstances throughout her career.

Pete Johnson, the penniless artist based on Owen Merton in the original manuscript, changed both his name and medium to become Alexander Williams, author of *The Burning Bush*, a novel of artistic merit which had received good reviews but sold poorly. His marriage collapses because of his incapacity to support his family; his wife leaves him, becomes a communist, then dies. At the end of the book, he is hopelessly compromised and defeated.

I took the physical aspects of manual labour from Grey Riddle

and wove them into a different story – a sort of my-version of
Hunger. This is my first, so to speak, Balzacian theme as it is
all money with love only incidental. It deals with the plight of
the artist in that sense, but also with the general plight of age.
As the chief protagonist is a writer I have had to show up the
conflict between business motives and art interests and pray
this is no bar to publisher's acceptance. I shall have a preface
saying that there are no actual publishers in it and the
publishers are victims of a system. I don't know whether I feel
myself or not, but I do feel I've 'said something' – also that it
is a natural step toward the French Revolution material. The
woman in my book becomes a Communist, but this is sympa-
thetically treated except as it would be criticised by quite
fanatical and stupid people. The man's salvation is in his
work. But the whole reaction in both instances is to find some
basis on which to establish life so that money won't destroy
you.

This synopsis, which Evelyn sent Lola, was amplified in the
preface to the book which also explained the narrative method.
Material in ordinary type represented conscious conclusions.
Italicised type and type in parentheses indicated internal conflict. Italics without parentheses represented thought which
arose by association and italics within parentheses represented
conflicts and decisions which had been determinedly ignored.
In spite of the apparent complexity of this method, the book is
eminently readable and clear in intent:

The stony corridor was chill and quiet ... (*like Napoleon's fort
... Kate screaming somewhere in the blackness when she touched
damp masonry.*) ... It terminated in a long apartment, like a
sort of undenominational chapel, in which prophylaxis rather
than adornment had preoccupied the decorator. Strips of
fiber matting had been laid between the rows of folding,
varnished chairs, like seats in movie theatres. The company
faced a glass partition, which allowed a prospect of dour,
enigmatic metal doors beyond, like doors of ovens or furnaces
...

*across the night, a line of fire sprang luridly ... stokers, disem-
barking, wore their overcoats – thermometer said ninety eight!* ...

The temperature is frigid here . . . *the management is saving coal!* . . . *tin mouth* . . . *tin windows* . . . He was dimly conscious of the wild, subhuman leap of his expectant nerves . . .

This passage, describing Alexander Williams' feelings as he awaits the cremation of his wife, demonstrates that Evelyn's descriptive intentions were clear enough. It was her philosophical intentions which perplexed the book's reviewers. The preface, after a few pages of statement of intent, soon moved on to Evelyn's obsession with the incompatibility of communism and free art. The argument was not pursued with much clarity – the reviewer of the Detroit *Free Press* commented, 'Politically, Mrs Scott is some kind of Marxist,' an observation which would have raised hackles when the review was forwarded by the clippings agency. Norman McLeod reviewed the book in a surprisingly favourable light for *New Masses* and, though he found the expressed interpretation of Marxism naive, he thought the book, 'a moving and serious effort to pose a contemporary human problem'. Dorothy Van Doren repeated the criticism she had made of *Eva Gay*, unaware that the real-life model for both characters was the same man: 'Mrs Scott [. . .] does not convince us that her artist is worth saving', a charge which could equally be levelled at Joyce's similarly self-obsessed Stephen Daedalus.

The main flaw of the book is its preface, inserted by Evelyn as a means of expounding ideas which could find no platform elsewhere. She was never quite satisfied with the novel, and amended her personal copy for a future revised edition. Though it was flawed in execution and marred by a largely irrelevant preface, the book stands as Evelyn's best thirties novel and, over-all, her most interesting experiment in prose.

The Clarksville visit must have been brief and no details are recorded of it. Maude Dunn still subsisted on charity, and now occupied a single room almost within sight of the grandiose mansion which had once been her home. Deserted by her husband and shamed by her only daughter, she had taken refuge in demanding from others the social deference which would have been hers automatically in her previous station in life. She may have been a sad victim of her social conditioning but she was by no means empty-headed. During her last two decades of life, she occupied herself translating *The Love-Life of Adrienne Lecouvreur*, a French novel by Cécile Sorel, and *O Sertao* by the Brazilian author Coelho Netto. Neither was ever published.

Evelyn was not remembered with affection by her former social peers in Clarksville and rumours of her activities since the elopement can have done little to enhance her estimation in their eyes. Awkward though the visit must have been for all concerned, it resulted in a remarkably affectionate portrayal of her native town. Almost alone among her books, *Background in Tennessee* lacks pessimism and morbidity. After twenty years of travel and almost thirty years' absence from Clarksville, she concluded that expatriation was a myth and that, over and above her consciousness as an American, she was, specifically, a Tennessean. Furthermore, she acknowledged that all her fundamental character formation had occurred during her Clarksville girlhood.

Such an admission raises several questions. To what extent was her frequently wilful behaviour the result of a conscious revolt and did it actually owe more to the imperiousness bred into a person reared in her class? And what percentage of her ideas on sexual freedom derived from Freud, feminism and the 'new woman', and how much was merely an extension of feminine coquetry, the actions of a Southern belle who did, rather than simply flirted?

Background in Tennessee does not attempt to answer these questions; unlike *Escapade*, it is almost devoid of subjective probing. Most reviewers were charmed by the book, though its formlessness was held against it and some commented on the peculiar Latinised syntax of her sentences. Her publisher made a vain attempt to get her to recast the book, a suggestion to which her response was predictably unfavourable. 'I regard style, structure and *even* punctuation as the affair of the author exclusively,' she countered and added, irrelevantly: 'I do not write for humourless revolutionaries.' The nature of the book, 'one-third biography, one-third local history and one-third opinions in general', in the words of one reviewer, confused critics. And in 1937, with the world moving toward war, an evocation of a turn of the century aristocratic childhood was not what the times demanded. Though generally reviewed well, it was not reviewed widely, a fact which Evelyn ascribed to a communist boycott against her. There is no evidence of this and the sympathetic treatment of *Bread and a*

Sword by *New Masses* suggests that, if the book was deliberately ignored, it was because it would not greatly interest a committed audience. She received more favourable attention from communist reviewers than from magazines representing Southern literature. *Bread and a Sword*, alone of her novels, was reviewed, dissected and found wanting in the *Southern Review*. Evelyn had a staunch ally in Paula Snelling of the *North Georgia Review*, who ended a survey of her work with a suggestion that she be considered for a Nobel Prize, but this was hardly representative of the main current of Southern opinion. *Background in Tennessee* portrayed a South which was not what the Northern intelligentsia wished to see depicted, nor was it the picture the Southern intelligentsia wished to have projected. As a result, the book's stature as a minor classic of its genre went unnoticed by Evelyn's literary contemporaries. In Clarksville, the local paper reviewed the book well. The prodigal was discreetly welcomed home.

25

Things Fall Apart

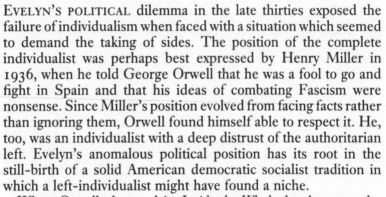

EVELYN'S POLITICAL dilemma in the late thirties exposed the failure of individualism when faced with a situation which seemed to demand the taking of sides. The position of the complete individualist was perhaps best expressed by Henry Miller in 1936, when he told George Orwell that he was a fool to go and fight in Spain and that his ideas of combating Fascism were nonsense. Since Miller's position evolved from facing facts rather than ignoring them, Orwell found himself able to respect it. He, too, was an individualist with a deep distrust of the authoritarian left. Evelyn's anomalous political position has its root in the still-birth of a solid American democratic socialist tradition in which a left-individualist might have found a niche.

When Orwell observed in *Inside the Whale* that by 1937 the whole of the intelligentsia was mentally at war, his analysis of a British situation was applicable to all parts of the Western world where free debate still prevailed. But in America, those who defended the fundamental human decencies which Orwell prized above dogma found themselves defending a vestigial liberalism which both sides declared irrelevant. Evelyn was no Orwell; she lacked, by virtue of her sex, temperament and sympathies, his identification with the frustrations and hopes of the ordinary man. Rather like Miller, she identified with aristocrats of the spirit, but unlike Miller, she could not walk away from the developing struggle.

Crisis was brewing in her personal life also. In June 1936 she had another serious quarrel with Lola Ridge, again ostensibly over the question of money. Evelyn had tried to assist her desperately poor friend several times and was always met with a proud rebuff. Though this disagreement was patched up, things were never the same again between the women.

When John Metcalfe came from England for a visit early in 1937, Evelyn met him in Montreal, and she was shocked by the visible deterioration in his appearance. The combination of physical illness and his neurotic sensibility had resulted in a complete mental collapse which had required hospitalisation. He had been discharged but was in a very agitated frame of mind and returned to England without Evelyn, who decided that she would not write to him until he had fully gained self-control. This was to take time, and circumstances kept the couple apart for several years to come.

The summer of 1937 was spent at a writers' conference in Boulder, Colorado, where, interviewed for a magazine, she found herself still remembered, doubtless to her great irritation, as the author of *The Narrow House*. She commented on that novel, 'Women weren't writing about the sort of things they are now, and they thought I was terrible. I was quite indignant about it. I didn't have the sense of humour I have now, I hope, so I wasted a lot of indignation on the desert air. I felt quite intellectually hifalutin about that book.' For the moment, she told her interviewer, her main interest was 'the future of art'.

For art to have a future, she felt that the rise of Marxist aesthetics must be combated. It was shortly after this interview that she took the unusual step of writing to public figures, often unknown to her, to canvass their opinions on the subject. Among these were Thomas Mann and Albert Einstein, to whom she sent unsolicited copies of *Bread and a Sword*, drawing attention to the ideas expressed in the preface. Both replied, politely, noncommittally and in German. Aldous Huxley sent a brief note intimating that the whole question was somewhat beneath him, but that he was not unsympathetic. For the first time since the early twenties she wrote to her former champion, Sinclair Lewis, who replied, 'I quite agree with you, and Dorothy Thompson agrees that there is apparently a very definite Stalinist conspiracy among the newspapers, magazines and publishing houses of New York to prevent or hamper the publication of anything at all criticising Communism.' However, he pointed out the obvious difficulty involved in exposing this.

Robert Hillyer, a poet, critic, Harvard professor and lifelong conservative, had come under communist pressure and Evelyn wrote to him suggesting some sort of anti-Stalinist grouping. Nothing came of this proposal, probably because Hillyer recognised in it an exaggerated and emotional response. 'We are both sensitive and highly strung people,' he wrote in reply, 'and for our own good we must beware of becoming obsessed with the situation.'

This warning came several years too late. A perfectly justifiable concern over political interference in literature had become obsessive, dangerously so when combined with a paranoiac cast of mind. As early as 1923, Waldo Frank had written in a letter, 'Suppose I pointed out a likeness between a mechanism in you and paranoia, would you say I had called you insane?' Occasionally Evelyn's letters would refer to her 'mild persecution complex' and a paranoiac interpretation was frequently applied to setbacks; to the fact that certain magazines would not print her work and to her problem-racked relations with all of her publishers. Paula Scott, Evelyn's daughter-in-law, thought that both Cyril and Creighton would have said that the seeds of an active paranoia were always present; seeds which began to sprout in the immediate prewar years.

In November 1938 Evelyn broadcast a five-minute talk on an NBC radio programme, *America Now*, which criticised sections of the American intelligentsia for justifying communist repression while simultaneously attacking Fascism and Nazism. In the same year she contributed a long article to a symposium, also entitled *America Now*, subtitled *An Enquiry into Civilisation in the United States by Thirty-Six Americans*. Both were well written and coherent, if strident in their tone. However, in 1939 she researched and wrote a long unpublished article on communist activities in the medical trades unions, dramatically entitled 'The Coming Struggle for Power through Medicine', which revealed, apart from a noticeable shift to the right in her opinions, a lack of clarity of expression and thought process. 'Liberals' and 'the left' are virtually equated and the existence of communists in medical trades unions is portrayed as evidence of an imminent takeover of society at large.

The *America Now* symposium was a repeat of a similar exercise carried out just after the First World War by the same editor, Harold Stearns. The prevailing mood of the earlier book was disgust with the commercialism of American life and a feeling that it was anathema to the creative process. Stearns evidently agreed and he became one of the first Americans to depart for Paris. There he achieved semi-legendary status as a literary bum and was portrayed in Hemingway's *The Sun Also Rises* as 'small heavy slow' Harvey Stone, who sat unshaven outside the literary cafés, seemingly dividing his time between drink and the race-track. It was this unlikely figure who invited a later generation of American intelligentsia to pronounce on civilisation and its discontents. The second symposium was noticeably less critical over-all than the first and Evelyn's contribution, categorised under 'Politics', not 'Arts', was the only one to criticise communism.

As well as continuous worry about John's mental state, this period also saw another serious attempt by the Clarksville relatives to unburden themselves of Mrs Dunn and this time Evelyn's cousins threatened to bring her to New York personally. The prospect rattled Evelyn, who seriously considered flight to England, but the threat passed, and no action was taken. She worked intermittently on the French Revolution novel and began to write what would be her last published book.

The Shadow of the Hawk was an idiosyncratic, though technically unexperimental, attempt at satire which, like her previous excursion into the genre with *Ideals*, was doomed by her deficient sense of humour. When Scribner published it in 1941 it had a small print run and met with mostly hostile notices. Clifton Fadiman in the *New Yorker* said that he thought *The Wave* to be the best Civil War novel ever written, but he found little merit in the latest perplexing offering. 'Miss Scott would appear to be fascinated by gray, mean people [...] Is it one of those imposing Dreiserian studies of the effects of society on character? Is it a lower middle-class satire, Dickens without humour? Does it purport to say trenchant things about justice and prison reform?' He may well have asked, though whatever the book was about, it was mercifully not anti-communism.

Its hero is Angus Pettigrew, son of a falsely convicted murderer. The theme, broadly stated, is the perennial Evelyn Scott concern: the incompatibility of human desires and social codes. Society is experienced in terms of grotesque caricature; a pseudo-religion called Yahootmaism emerges, crank charities such as the Crime Improvement Fund and the Convict Kiddie Culture Group attempt to alleviate Pettigrew's distress and a series of characters with names such as Judge Prentiss Porkley, Dinty Duggan, Dr Frankus Sandow and Mrs Martha Whipple Thurkle Paget Porter French McGee take the stage. The justifying ingredients of either humour or Swiftian disgust are absent and the novel must be counted as one of Evelyn's least successful books.

In 1939, with money problems once more, Evelyn accepted her only job beside writing, as an instructor at Skidmore College on a fortnight per month basis. She enjoyed teaching, though she found the internal politics of higher education irksome. There was a quota of faculty Marxists with whom she dealt, she claimed, quite amicably and a quota of dim students whose lack of perception drove her to distraction. Most disturbing of all was the growing war fever, which she reported in a letter to Theodore Dreiser: 'Every kid here believes in war with heartfelt enthusiastic conviction. They are all waiting eagerly to see it happen in 1939 when they will attain the romance that distinguished the pasts of their parents and become lost generations able to say at first hand how dreadful war is.'

Communication with Dreiser had been reopened in May 1938 when Evelyn wrote to him on the question of communism. She said she had learned in 1930 of communist plans to boycott the reviewing of non-communist books and claimed that, after publication of *Bread and a Sword*, she had been warned that she would be 'taken for a ride' and boycotted out of existence. She was convinced that this was the reason for the sparse reviewing of *Background in Tennessee*, and invited Dreiser to join her anti-Stalinist grouping, a proposal he deftly fended. In spite of periods of fellow-travelling, she informed him that his books were now under a boycott also.

If this were the case, Dreiser replied, he had not heard of it. Though he may have been out of favour with hard-liners, he was still sufficiently committed to be active in various anti-Fascist groups. He fully approved of the idea of communism, though not necessarily of the dictates which the Party handed down. Evelyn and Dreiser met in New York before she left for Skidmore and Dreiser apparently swore at her for half an hour in front of the George Washington Hotel. This restored their relationship to the cordial feud which had run through the twenties and culminated in Evelyn's telling him, in 1929, that he was the rudest man she had ever met.

She wrote to him amicably in January 1939, mostly on her teaching experiences, but also complaining that 'I seem to be having all my excitement about free speech and free art all by myself; a campaign carried on by myself for myself to rouse myself to saying more aloud to myself what I have already told myself I believe enough to die for. Except I don't want to die for anything as long as I can live for it.'

Her faith in Dreiser was shattered by his *Thoreau*, in which he seemed to suggest that the ends justified the means, no matter whether the means involved violence or chicanery. In April 1939 she wrote a recriminatory letter on the subject, the last communication between them. She described herself, for the first and last time, as a 'Christian Socialist' and asserted that the means and the ends must be identical: '[...] a man is as he does; his cause no more just than his everyday acts.' Very uncharacteristically, religion crept into her argument: 'I love those that serve "God" and not "Power".' She ended: 'I feel someone is trying to injure you. You can't have written the mimeograph.'

But write it he had. Dreiser, the twelfth of thirteen children born to a poor family, who had spent his teens drifting from one menial job to another, had more reason than most to be sceptical of American capitalism, having experienced its workings from the bottom. Like many self-made men, his thinking was too individual to be yoked to a party line but, with an apparent showdown between Fascism and communism imminent, he appears to have concluded that the niceties of liberalism or even 'Christian Socialism' were dispensable. For Evelyn it was a deep betrayal, to which she reacted in a way which foreshadowed her interpretation of other future 'betrayals'. Someone, unknown, was tampering with Dreiser's work, a conclusion which found its echo in future accusations of theft, conspiracy and editorial interference. In a poem written after the break she described Dreiser as lying to her 'with blandly self-important face'. His heroic stature had been shattered.

No survey of Evelyn's life in these years can avoid her apparent blindness to European events. Even the Soviet–German pact, which might well have reinforced her views on the identical nature of both state repressions, passes unmentioned in her letters. Her sense of the 'communist threat' did not extend much further than the narrow world of the North-Eastern intelligentsia, most of whom, with every justification, were far more worried about Fascism than communism. It was a world in which Fascists were scarce: a survey on the Spanish Civil War yielded only one Franco supporter. Yet, such was her solipsism that she could not extend her field of vision beyond the area in which she earned her daily bread. In her defence it might be argued that this avoided the distant espousal of causes which, on closer examination, prove vile and repressive, but the solitary nature of her crusade indicates that this, of all times, was the wrong time to wage it. A few years later and even diehard rightist critics of Russia would be temporarily silent. As Europe entered into war, Evelyn was alone, ignored, and increasingly prey to delusions that she had been specially singled out for persecution and suppression. Her voyage in the dark had begun.

26

Into the Tunnel

ON THE OUTBREAK of war, John had been drafted into the RAF and, since he was too old for active duty, was assigned to the task of training pilots. Evelyn made plans to join him in England in 1940 but was defeated by a lack of funds and the long-drawn-out terminal illness of her mother. She visited Clarksville several times to see her, but was not present when Maude Dunn died in late April 1940.

A few years earlier, Evelyn wrote that the sight of her mother affected her like a helpless rabbit she had once seen and wished there had been some way to end its sufferings painlessly. She lived with the fear, expressed in *Escapade* and sometimes in letters, of becoming like her mother, a passive victim of an apparently hostile world. Maude Dunn's genetic influence pre-dominated in her, and the threat that she might be forced to live with her had haunted Evelyn for many years.

In death Mrs Dunn showed a fortitude of spirit and a dignity which the cruel events of her life had done their best to destroy. Evelyn wrote:

> Yes, Lola, dear, losing mother did strange things to the emotions and still does. Death is a wonderful clarifier of feeling. Mother was so oddly, too, both the same hen-headed person she always was, and quite different toward the end of her life. When she was ill, she had the most really aristocratic dignity and reticence. I don't think she ever complained except occasionally in a rather sharp joking way; and the only time she

was furiously angry was when some nosey church members who didn't know her butted into her room. I was there and she quashed them far better than I could in a highly dignified way, although she was so ill. Her face changed, too; and got a curious aquiline contour, different from the one it had when the bones didn't show. And she always thought I did everything for her, whether I did or not — other people got no credit for their flowers, these all came from me. It was very touching. So I knew in the end that I really did love her, and that seeming not to was an instinct of nature in defence against a temperament too unlike my own to be lived with. It was my piece of sentiment to arrange what was to be read at her funeral, even though I couldn't be there. They read the Episcopal service at the cemetery, and Saint Paul on charity and the last chapter of Ecclesiastes, those being the loveliest things I know. So I hoped the petty little townsfolk would hear about charity for once. I don't like rationalistic funerals, in which death and garbage collection are on a par.

Relations with Lola had worsened, and letters between the two women were infrequent. Lola Ridge was moving toward a crisis of her own which would be resolved in 1941 when she died, probably by her own hand, after years of semi-invalidism. These were bad years for delicate sensibilities. In 1941 Charlotte Wilder, sister of Thornton, a poet and a good friend of Evelyn's, was incarcerated in Belle Vue Psychiatric Hospital, where she remained for many years. A few years later, Dreiser committed suicide.

It was around this time that Evelyn's progressive paranoia became more pronounced, and her statements on politics crossed the delicate line separating crankishness from irrationality. Her suspicions of communism expanded to include the whole spectrum of the left which, she felt, was conspiring toward the creation of a sinister global control system. She began to complain of surveillance by the government, by Works Progress Administration agents and other representatives of shadowy, unnamed organisations.

There are a number of reasons why she might have attracted the attention of national security agencies. She had been conspicuously outspoken at a time of national hysteria and had associated with many known communists. She had been a close friend of Emma Goldman and had actively lobbied for her readmission to America. Her lifelong friend and sometime patron, Margaret de Silver, had taken as her second husband the Italian anarchist Carlo Tresca, a man only marginally less notorious than Emma Goldman.

However, a search I instituted under the Freedom of Information and Privacy Act revealed that she had never been the subject of investigation by the FBI. What it did turn up was a letter sent to that agency by Evelyn on the caretaker of her apartment block whom she believed to be an enemy agent. The excisions in the letter were made by the FBI. It is dated November 27, 1940:

In the course of an interview with ***** who is investigating subversive activities on the WPA art projects, I asked advice about the incidents I relate below: two conversations with ***** in the house where I now have a room. ***** thought the remarks made to me by this man sufficiently suspicious in character to be passed on to you, for your judgement on their possible importance in indicating some subversive connection.

*****'s name is *****. He says he is a Belgian, and used to be a sailor. He has been in this country for sometime, he says; and from my observation and that of friends who have stayed in the same building, is conscientious and hard-working. However, he is very slow-witted, speaks poor English, and is almost illiterate: the kind of man, in short, who could easily be exploited by others.

I was here last winter, and had nothing to complain of, and he said nothing on the subject of politics. However, when I returned in September after a summer in Saratoga, his first remark to me, on my arrival, was that I would 'never see my husband' (who is in the RAF in England) again. I asked why he said such a thing, and he told me he had a 'Belgian friend' who was on a ship, who came here sometimes and told him what was happening in England and Europe. I cannot convey the conversation in the man's precise words, but he was evidently convinced that England was already conquered by Hitler. He further said a great deal about the power of the German army, insisted that Mussolini's soldiers were 'already here' (in America?) and that within an indefinite period but possibly 'inside a year', what was happening 'over there' (in Europe?) would have started in this country. He advised me to give up any expectation of rejoining my husband ever, because he said the 'trouble' here would eventually prevent my husband's getting to me. In concluding this conversation, he told me that the 'poor have to get together against the rich'. This it seemed was to happen whenever the trouble he mentioned started. He said he had a 'place to go' at that time, and that I could go there with him if I wanted to escape what would occur in New York.

I mentioned the above incident on the first visit of ***** with ***** from the WPA, but because my own unpleasant experiences then (?) under discussion seemed to point to *haeckling* by people in Communist dominated unions connected with publishing and the arts, the possible connections suggested by a second incident last week were not apparent.

A man arrived here one afternoon as I was returning to the house, and as I entered the hall, this man who came without baggage, was greeted by ***** as 'my friend' from 'far off'. Being already interested in the story of the Belgian, I wondered if this were he, as he seemed to have left his belongings in *****'s care. This man was here three days (I think), and occupied a room next to that of a friend who is living here and knows of the first incident. This friend, *****, asked ***** if the visitor in the room next to hers were his Belgian acquaintance. He said the man was not, but was ***** then came to me on some other pretext connected with ***** and delivered an excited jumbled account of the visitor (who, by this time, seemed to have departed). It would be impossible to repeat, verbatim, what ***** meant to convey, but it sounded something like the sort of thing you read of as having happened in Norway and elsewhere when German occupation of the country was *immanent*. All I can say definitely (****'s English becomes only half *intelligible* when he is excited), is that the arrival of armies was mentioned; and that he said there would be a false announcement of 'Peace' over the radio, whenever what was supposed to happen did. He said other people would assume the announcement genuine, but that he would know it was not. His 'friend' (I think he meant the man who had just left), he said, was ***** and I gathered the 'friend' was in some way connected with all this information and with *****'s own intention to escape 'the trouble' by leaving New York.

I asked *****'s advice before writing, because it seemed fantastic that any genuine conspirator should trust a man so stupid and evidently indiscreet with serious plans. However, as an additional fact that may have a bearing on whatever the situation is, I may say that ***** is reputed to be a German-American. I don't know anyone who has ever seen him, but ***** has met his wife, who comes here sometimes *****. He is said to live in ***** to whom ***** referred was not called ***** by him, although of course he may have been that gentleman.

The letter was addressed to Edgar J. Hoover (*sic*), the man whose first act of consequence, as a Department of Justice official, had been the deportation from America of Emma Goldman. The one-time radical had become an FBI stool-pigeon.

Her letter bears all the hallmarks of a crank missive. The caretaker may have been a man with a mordant sense of humour, or may himself have been slightly deranged. An element of sexual innuendo is present in his insistence that she would never see John again, coupled with his offer to be her protector when the trouble started. It could only have caused an evidently stupid man problems which, arguably, he may well have deserved, but the likelihood is that, as one of thousands of flimsy allegations received by the agency, it was filed on the off-chance of future developments and forgotten.

A more serious point is raised by Evelyn's admission that she had already been talking to officials of the Works Progress Adminstration on the subject of 'subversion' within that organisation. Whatever the content of these conversations, it appears not to have reached the ears of the FBI. In later years, Creighton alleged that his mother wrote frequently to that agency, but this evidently deluded letter is the only one on file and, it is safe to assume, her only contact with them.

Prevented by circumstance from working on the French Revolution novel, *Before Cock Crow*, Evelyn began work on a book set in the New York theatre world at the turn of the century. Much of the material was based on reminiscences by her Saratoga Springs landlady, Mrs Rodman, who had been an actress before retiring to run a tea shop and boarding house. The manuscript version of this unpublished novel exhibits the same faults as that of *Before Cock Crow*; rambling long sentences burdened to incomprehensibility by subclauses, and an extreme length disproportionate to the interest of the plot. The final draft of *Escape into Living*, as the book was finally called, is close to a thousand pages of typescript.

The Shadow of the Hawk was published in 1941, to an indifference Evelyn ascribed to boycott and conspiracy, but which probably owed much to the fact that there were few years less propitious for fiction publication. Her career as an author ended with this book, which was issued in a 'token' edition of around five hundred. By this time she was living in Clinton, Ontario, where she had rejoined John, who had been posted there. Here she underwent a strange, brief conversion to Catholicism. Creighton had introduced her to several Jesuits of his acquaintance, in the hope of staving off the mental collapse toward which she seemed headed. His old friend Tom Merton had, by now, taken his monastic vows and Creighton was intellectually curious as to the pull of the Church upon his boyhood companion. His dialogue with the Jesuits came to nothing, but in 1941 Evelyn was received into the Roman Catholic Church.

Her conversion lasted a mere nine months. She came to regret it and claimed that her rapid apostasy resulted from priestly objections to her divorce. Since her 'marriage' to Cyril was unrecognised by civil law, and certainly unrecognised by the Catholic Church, this is highly unlikely. In Ontario, the manuscript of *Before Cock Crow* was allegedly stolen from her rooms, the first of a number of 'thefts' of her writing which she would claim in the coming years.

John was posted back to England and in the autumn of 1943 Evelyn joined Creighton and his new wife, Paula, at Tappan, New Jersey. Creighton had been exempted from military service and was working there as a news editor, painting in his free time. The flat was tiny and Paula Scott remembers Evelyn's stay as being fraught with tension. Her daily behaviour had by now reached a level of irrationality which made life all but impossible for those around her. She was unable to rejoin John until much bureaucratic formality had been completed and her mental state did not make this any easier.

She arrived in London in 1944, and endured the last of the London bombings. Until 1947, nothing is known of her activities. It is clear that she suffered great mental and physical hardship for, when the dust of war settled, the woman who emerged from the long dark tunnel bore no resemblance to the free spirit who, in the aftermath of the First World War, had exulted in the rebellion of Greenwich Village.

27
The Family as Nightmare - 2

IN APRIL 1947 Witter Bynner received a letter from Evelyn written from the basement flat of a house at 26 Belsize Crescent, Hampstead, London. This had been bought by John and split into flats; the remainder of the house was occupied by refugee tenants. It was John's intention that this would provide a subsistence income but, as a rent freeze had been imposed by the new Labour government, the profession of landlord was not a lucrative one. John had been demobbed from the RAF and had returned to teaching. A new novel of his, *All Friends Are Strangers*, was about to be published.

The postwar letters differ markedly from those of the interwar years. Most of the latter give the impression of having been written spontaneously, are frequently undated, often without a return address, and exist simply to record an evanescent mood. Of the surviving correspondence, only that with Emma Goldman gives any sense that its author felt posterity might be looking over her shoulder.

Postwar letters are invariably dated and are usually headed by the address of both sender and recipient. Often they are marked 'Personal'. Their language is quasi-legal or vituperative, and the margins are filled with addenda, afterthoughts and comments. Political paranoia alternates with desperately sad requests for assistance to re-establish a career cut short by the machinations of her enemies. To Bynner she wrote:

Your letters of February 4th, also duly received, assured me that you had been there in the interim, but in it you speak of the possibility of going to the United States for a while, for a 'cure' for the various maladies; and you may be there now, so I shall send the original of this to the USA and the carbon to Chapala, and shall be obliged to have both acknowledged, and very good if with that, is news of your having got rid of all the damnable ailments, notwithstanding the rotten riddling of the medical profession by politics – which I think shameful as I am still convinced we must have genuine science and not god-damn hocus pocus, if we are to be genuinely healed instead of just 'experimented on', like a lot of damn political guinea pigs – and to hell with em! The truth about that has got to be told and the sooner the better.

I have had plenty of the same or parallel and am so completely disgusted I don't patronise medicine at all, having too much respect for the best in science to risk the worst, as we are all liable to until the 'totes' are put out of commission.

The 'totes' – totalitarians – was a category including the British Labour Party and a variety of other organisations; at times, the United Nations and the Brazilian secret service had now become the enemy. She complained frequently of unanswered letters resulting from 'tote' interference, but this patently was due to their unbalanced content. Ironically most of the letters she sent attempting to revive her literary career could only have had the opposite effect and, to any hard-pressed editor, ignoring them would have seemed the simplest and most humane response.

William Rose Benet, formerly a fringe member of the twenties Village crowd, was, in 1948, an editor on the *Saturday Review of Literature*. Through his influence the magazine published a poem of Evelyn's on her mother's death in which her name was inadvertently spelt Dunne. Evelyn demanded a correction to the true spelling, Dunn, and ascribed the error to a plot on her stepmother's part to deprive her of a probably non-existent paternal inheritance. Benet circulated a sheaf of Evelyn's verse to a number of magazines which rejected them and, when he returned the manuscripts explaining this, the correspondence abruptly ceased. This was, she felt, evidence of a conspiracy in operation and not their lack of quality. Benet did his best out of old loyalties, as did Lewis Gannett, but to the emerging postwar literary generation she was an anachronism known, if at all, as a name from the past. Her enthusiasm for work other than John Metcalfe's and her own had died and nowhere in the postwar letters is there reference to any new writer or literary trend that excited her. Instead there is constant reiteration of old injuries and slights all of which – the financial failure of publishers, paper rationing, her failure to achieve republication or to have new work accepted, and the ignoring of her unanswerable letters – further fuelled her paranoia.

She became what she always feared, a mirror image of her mother. Yet the demands of Maude Dunn on her only daughter were mild in comparison with those made by Evelyn on her only son. After the disastrous stay at Tappan in 1943, Creighton saw her only once, on a forty-eight-hour stopover in London in 1949. Shortly after this he stopped writing personally and the task of maintaining the correspondence fell to his wife Paula. It was his intention to keep his mother, who showed every desire wilfully to interfere with his life, firmly at arm's length, as she had kept her own. Creighton worked for a succession of radio broadcasting companies and never left forwarding addresses when he moved. Undaunted, Evelyn would learn the name of his new company, then bombard his superiors with unbalanced letters about the conspiracy which was keeping her son from writing to her.

These complaints, with their allegations of 'sinister influences', could be ignored while he worked for domestic radio stations in America. However, in the late forties he worked for Radio Free Europe, a propaganda station based in Germany aimed at Eastern Europe. The station was under virtual CIA control and any hint of political or social unorthodoxy was not regarded leniently. This was more the case when, in 1955, he began work for the International Cooperation Agency in Saigon. These were the years of Greene's *The Quiet American*, and CIA activity in Saigon and surveillance of American personnel there were exceptionally intense. It was no help to have a mother who wrote, according to Creighton, to the American Ambassador, to John Foster Dulles, and even to President Eisenhower on the subject of totalitarian pressures which were keeping her apart from her son. Yet, for whatever reason, the ties which linked him to his mother prevented him from making a clean break with her until many years later, by which time the damage was done, and it was all too late.

Stranded in England under a Labour administration to which she was highly unsympathetic, Evelyn's position became increasingly hopeless. John's teaching salary was low and their outgoings on the house were high. Poverty reduced her to wearing rags, and to a state of near toothlessness. Neighbouring children in Hampstead taunted her and called her 'the old witch'. Politically she now called herself a Churchillian Conservative in England, and a Republican in American terms. Her letters were dotted with xenophobic and anti-semitic comments and she became insistent on acknowledgement of her status as an American citizen 'of many generations' standing'. In terms of her youthful feelings, she fulfilled Dorothy Parker's terrible dictum, 'You become what you most despise'. Her reversion to ancestral type was complete.

Publication of Cyril's autobiography in 1943 was in America only and Evelyn did not receive a copy until 1947. She was shocked by what she saw as distortions in his portrayal of their years together and wrote a long document, circulated to friends, titled *A Précis of Events Indicative of Libel*. As usual, sinister influences were to blame. In many ways, the memoir is very circumspect regarding Evelyn and the distortions were indicative of a man at the end of his tether, rather than wilful fabrications. The book ends in 1934, almost ten years before publication. After this both Cyril and Creighton worked for a time on a Works Progress Administration scheme, but afterward he settled into retirement. He married once more in the fifties, losing his wife several years later, and died in 1960, aged 88. He became increasingly more involved with the Wellman family, readopted his old name and, after the mid-thirties, he and Evelyn did not meet and no letters passed between them.

John and Evelyn's main literary friendship in postwar London was with John Gawsworth, then editor of *Poetry Review*. Evelyn contributed a poem and three articles on American poetry to the magazine: lucid but unremarkable, they were her last appearances in print. Gawsworth was a central figure in London literary life and a particular friend of John, who was to appoint him as his literary executor.

The main hope of the couple, certainly at least of Evelyn, was a return to America. John had made a brief visit to New York in

1947, necessary for his entry quota status, during which he had attempted and failed to find teaching work. In 1951 Margaret de Silver began a fund to allow the couple to return to America. Signatories of the original draft appeal were Waldo Frank, Dawn Powell, Allen Tate, Lewis Gannett, John Dos Passos and Edmund Wilson. This was eventually successful, though there were a good number of refusals from people who had been annoyed by Evelyn's behaviour and some inexplicable omissions. William Faulkner's name was included on the list, then mysteriously struck off and, though William Carlos Williams was happy to make a donation, he did not want his name used.

Debts in London were mounting frighteningly and a small grant from the Institute of Arts and Letters was soon absorbed by creditors. Attempts to sell the flat were hampered by the fact that two of the three flats were let at uneconomic rents, and the fund was their last chance of return. Sufficient money was raised for a return passage in 1953 and as a stopgap it was arranged that they stay at the Huntingdon Hartford Foundation at Pacific Palisades, California. The flat was sold at a loss and, in March 1953, the couple crossed the Atlantic for the last time.

28

Home - 2

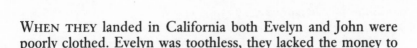

WHEN THEY landed in California both Evelyn and John were poorly clothed. Evelyn was toothless, they lacked the money to pay an excess baggage charge and their luggage was impounded.

The couple were to stay at the Foundation for over a year. There were further allegations of theft of papers and manuscripts and the possibility of a move east was held up by Evelyn's poor health. She experienced a number of heart attacks while at the Foundation but, when she had sufficiently recovered, she and John sailed for New York where they planned to locate an apartment near Columbia University.

Finally they settled in the Benjamin Franklin Hotel, a residential establishment on the upper West Side which offered communal kitchen facilities to supplement the room and bathroom. Many residents were refugees and the hotel was situated in what was known as 'the refugee belt'. As if it were threatened by this, Evelyn proclaimed her American identity more stridently. John soon found work teaching in a boys' prep school, a job he was to lose after some years because of his increasingly evident drink problem. This also affected the tutoring hours, arranged through an agency, which became his sole means of supporting himself and Evelyn. But the quality of his writing was undiminished and he continued to publish. *My Cousin Geoffrey* was published in England in 1956 and in New York he gained the approval of August Delerth, the publisher of, and collaborator with, H. P. Lovecraft. Delerth considered Metcalfe to be one of the modern masters of the macabre and published an excellent novella, *The Feasting Dead*, and several equally powerful short stories in the anthologies issued by his company, Arkham House. Despite poverty, John still annually sent money to maintain his membership of the Savile Club in London.

He had kept a diary for much of his life; a record of surface minutiae which offers no glimpse, except what can be inferred, of his interior state. He was so meticulous that the record, 'Drinks. Supper. Bed.' which closes most journal entries is often seen to have been written in the ink of the next day's entry. The diaries of 1955 reveal a slightly eccentric elderly couple, frequently ill, poor, but not destitute, sharing a life of near-retirement in which shopping expeditions and meals are the main daily events:

Saturday, January 22, 1955.
Snow again, – melting later.
  Breakfast; after which E. & I walked to picture-framers with Jig's picture, but found shop not yet open. Got cigarettes and collected laundry on the way back. Smoked etc.
  Went out twice for food (second time just after jar of coffee broken). Had coffee and then another try with Jig's picture, this time successfully. Price to be $9 and ready in 'about ten days'. (Mintz, 411 Amsterdam Avenue). Came back. Warmer (about 34°). Smoked etc.
  Lunch and nap.
  Bought drinks.
  Stella Ballantine, due at 6, arrived at about 6.20. Drinks and talk. Dinner 'at home' of steak, lemon meringue pie, cheese, coffee.
  Stella B. stayed till about 11.15, and E & I did not get to bed, after, till around 1.

This records a particularly active day, and often there is a simple statement, 'Quiet day at hotel', or 'School as usual'. Stella Ballantine, Emma Goldman's niece and literary heir, remained a friend as did Margaret de Silver. Others kept Evelyn at a cordial distance, if they had not already fallen out with her. Lewis Gannett received one too many denunciatory letters and ceased communication in the late fifties. He saw her only once in that decade, at Margaret de Silver's apartment, and was amazed by the outward appearance of calm and charm she maintained in contrast to the hysteria of her letters. However, he was to observe sadly, everyone who had been even slightly involved with her had been eventually exasperated. There was no lack of goodwill among former friends, but many were grappling with their own problems. In the aftermath of McCarthy, both Waldo Frank and Kay Boyle were under a cloud of suspicion and Kay Boyle's husband had lost his job on account of his wife's alleged communist sympathies.

Other allies, who had not undergone years of exasperation, came forward with help. One was Louise Bogan, a poet and former slight acquaintance, to whom Evelyn had written for help in getting her work republished. At 58, Louise Bogan was only four years younger than Evelyn, and had herself suffered a number of mental breakdowns. Yet the contrast between the two women could not have been greater and, far from being trapped in the past, Louise Bogan was aware of, and fascinated by, emerging currents in literature. Shortly after her re-encounter with Evelyn, she travelled to San Francisco where she witnessed some of the early public readings of the Beat Generation. John's diary records that the meeting with Evelyn took place on October 18, 1955, and Louise Bogan gave her own description in a letter to her friend, May Sarton:

[...] I had a sad and rather eerie meeting, early this week, with poor old Evelyn Scott. I say *old* advisedly, since she really has fallen into the dark and dank time – the time I used to fear so much when I was in my thirties. She is old because she has failed to grow – up, in, on ... So that at 62 she is not only frayed and dingy (she must have been a beauty in her youth) but silly and more than a little mad. She met me only casually, years ago, with Charlotte Wilder, but now, of course, she thinks I can *do* something for her – so transparent, poor thing. She is not only in the physical state I once feared, but she is living in the blighted area of the West 70's, near Broadway: that area which absorbs the queer, the old, the failures, into furnished or hotel rooms, and adds gloom to their decay. It was all there! She took me out to a grubby little tea-room around the corner, insisted on paying for the tea, and brought out, from time to time, from folds in her apparel, manuscripts that will never see print. I never *was* able to read her, even in her hey-day, and her poetry

now is perfectly terrible. Added to all this, she is in an active state
of paranoia – things and people are her enemies; she has been
plotted against in Canada, Hampstead, New York and California; her manuscripts have been stolen, time and time again, etc.,
etc. – We should thank God, that we remain in our senses! As
you know, I really fear mad people; I have some attraction for
them because talent is a kind of obverse of the medal. I must,
therefore, detach myself from E.S. I told her to send the MS to
Grove Press, and that is all I can do. 'But I must know the
editor's name!', she cried. 'I can't chance having my poems fall
into the hands of some secretary' ... O dear, O dear ...

Louise Bogan did not detach herself from ES, but remained a
friend until her death, afterwards helping the emotionally shattered John Metcalfe. Kay Boyle proved to be another good friend.
Despite their forty years of intermittent friendship by letter, she
saw much more of Evelyn during her last decade than she did
when both were expatriates. Though sympathetic with Evelyn's
plight, she did not view John with much affection. 'I found him
very defensive, apparently deeply humiliated by their situation in
this house-keeping hotel on the West Side in New York City. He
was most unattractive physically, very ego-oriented, and had a
very hectic manner,' she recalled. She could not offer material
assistance since she and her husband were fighting a court case
against his expulsion from the US Foreign Service, a case they
eventually won. Both were living in Connecticut where Kay Boyle
worked as a teacher. Evelyn's postwar right-wing sympathies
stopped short of McCarthy and Kay Boyle recalled that conversations in the last months of Evelyn's life were often about the
evils of that officially sanctioned paranoiac vision.
    The mid-fifties saw several hopeful signs of a revival in
Evelyn's career. The Definition Press, a small publishing
company dedicated mostly to spreading the philosophical ideas of
poet-turned-thaumaturge, Eli Siegel, expressed interest in
reprinting *A Calendar of Sin*. Siegel had reviewed the book warmly
on its appearance, and was of the opinion that it was the greatest
novel ever written by a woman. Granville Hicks, a former communist opponent of Evelyn's, who had since recanted, recommended the same book to Macmillan. A revival was doubtless
hindered by the book's enormous length and nothing came of

either attempt. There was a plan to reissuue *The Wave*, to which Caroline Gordon offered to write an introduction, but this too floundered. Robert Welker, a young graduate student from Clarksville, was engaged in a doctoral study of Evelyn's work, the only one to date that has been made. She still held hopes of gaining a publisher for *Escape into Living* and worked intermittently on the French Revolution novel which had started life twenty years earlier. Scribner, having despaired of its delivery, cancelled their contract in 1952.

It was as a forgotten woman subsisting on the lowest rung of genteel poverty that Evelyn spent the last decade of her life. Her mental condition fluctuated but does not seem to have deteriorated or improved over-all. An otherwise lucid letter to Paula Scott, written in 1960, is suddenly punctuated by the following question:

> Does this damn enemy sound-racket bother you there? I don't know whether anything is ever officially said about it, but I owes every American with a mind an undemnity for the nusiance it gets away with, due to the fact that sound is conveyed by this war weapon to one brain at a time electrically, and someone can be in the same room with a victim and hear nothing the other fellow hears.
>
> Remember I told you this and am responsible. The use of this war-weapon on many citizens and subjects – for it was a pest when we were in England too – is enough in itself to justify our Declaration of War, and is hard on health everywhere.

In the light of such claims it is difficult to know what credence can be given to Evelyn's statements in these years. According to Dr May Mayers, her physician for many years, there was little wrong with the heart which Evelyn often claimed to be seriously weak. Evelyn also asserted that she suffered from voices in the head and from expressive aphasia, the inability to express thought in words or to understand thoughts expressed by others. This may explain the 'enemy sound-racket', but there is no way of knowing whether these diagnoses were made by a doctor or whether, like the weak heart, they were a product of Evelyn's hypochondriac imagination.

In ironic repetition of Evelyn's relations with her own mother, Creighton and Paula Scott lived in fear that she might descend on them in California, where they were living. He had completely lost patience with his mother and, because of an adverse testimony given to a Senate sub-committee on misuse of foreign aid, was jobless and extremely poor. At the hearing, forty of his mother's letters were produced in evidence against him. In spite of a disjointed education which left him without even a high school diploma, he had forged a career for himself which was now in ruins. Never to work again, he died in 1965, occupying his days writing a memoir of childhood which judged his mother in the bitterest terms. He saw her present condition as merely a grotesque exaggeration of the egoism and self-willedness which were constants in her life. Communications stopped completely in 1960 and neither he nor Paula attended Evelyn's funeral.

John Metcalfe's health was further ravaged by a cerebral haemorrhage in 1960 which left him unable to write for two full years. In March 1963 he reported that Evelyn was very ill, and that he was about to be hospitalised and receive ECT treatment for an unspecified mental disorder.

Evelyn's illness was diagnosed as lung cancer. By now a chain-smoker and suffering from a hacking cough, she entered hospital and was operated upon. John confided his anxieties to Lewis Gannett:

July 14, 1963
We seem to be coming to the end of the Evelyn Scott–John Metcalfe trail – tho' I do still v. sincerely hope not.

She is in the Francis Delafield, – has been for five weeks under x-ray – and I expect her home in a week or so. She will then report to the clinic monthly, – and, later, the x-raying may be renewed.

It is difficult, at present, to imagine life without her, and I *hope* I needn't.

Everyone, of course, is now out of town and life in this hotel is dreadful. The kind of thing one props up in bars is no good, and I need someone different [...] I wish I could *see* you, Lewis. I am v. unhappy [...] E. is v. liberal and maintains a sense of proportion as to all human frailties [...]

August 6, 1963
Just a line to tell you that darling Evelyn died on Aug. 3rd, and
is being buried today.
What is there to say . . .

Evelyn was released from hospital on August 3 and died that
night in her sleep beside John. The convoluted path, begun in a
Clarksville mansion, the romantic elopement and triumph over
setback, the career filled with such promise in the Village of the
early twenties when Art was proclaimed as the new religion, had
come to this miserable end.

John Metcalfe was distraught and rendered helpless by his wife's
death. Louise Bogan reported in January 1964 that he was in
great need and probably taking more refuge in whisky than was
good for him. She obtained medical help and wrote on his behalf
to the Carnegie Fund for Authors. Eventually he was committed
to a New York mental hospital, from which he wrote to John
Gawsworth of his wish to 'lie in English soil'.

Margaret de Silver, who had helped so much in the past, had
died in 1962 and the task of helping John fell to her son Burnham
and his wife Claire. They, and others, lobbied the British Consu-
late and toward the end of 1964 they succeeded in getting John
discharged and repatriated to England.

The diary of his final year of life is as bland and self-effacing as
his earlier ones. It chronicles his high intake of alcohol, also the
heavy dosages of prescribed tranquillisers he combined with it in
a dangerous mixture. His chief drinking companion was John
Gawsworth who was also confirmed on an alcoholic course. On
July 28, 1965 Metcalfe stumbled down the stairs of the London
rooming house in which he was staying and died, without regain-
ing consciousness, three days later. He is buried at Mill Hill
Cemetery.

Gawsworth had been appointed as his literary executor but he
proved incapable, perhaps because of his own chronic alco-
holism, of promoting his work assiduously. Gawsworth was
reduced to homelessness before his death and the fate of several
copyrights entrusted to him remains a mystery. He survived
Metcalfe by only five years.

After Gawsworth's death, John's literary estate found its way on to the London rare book market. There exists a lively market for literature of the macabre and his books and manuscripts found ready buyers. This was not the case with the books and manuscripts of Evelyn's work which he brought to London with him: after languishing on the shelves of a metropolitan book dealer for a number of years, they were consigned to a storeroom at the back of the shop and forgotten.

When the bookshop gained a new partner it was decided that the storeroom should be cleared so its contents were sold to a friend of one of the owners, the mildly eccentric proprietor of a junkshop situated on the fringe of a Yorkshire mill town.

Coda

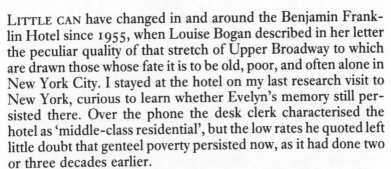

LITTLE CAN have changed in and around the Benjamin Franklin Hotel since 1955, when Louise Bogan described in her letter the peculiar quality of that stretch of Upper Broadway to which are drawn those whose fate it is to be old, poor, and often alone in New York City. I stayed at the hotel on my last research visit to New York, curious to learn whether Evelyn's memory still persisted there. Over the phone the desk clerk characterised the hotel as 'middle-class residential', but the low rates he quoted left little doubt that genteel poverty persisted now, as it had done two or three decades earlier.

There were few transients in this residential hotel. It must have housed about five hundred guests, most past retirement age. A core of around twenty congregated daily on the vinyl settees of the lobby, conversing in broken dialogues of non sequiturs, often in accents which revealed that this was still the refugee belt. The barely furnished rooms had a lively, varied insect population and the best to be said about it as a place of residence was that it was cheap.

Here I worked on a revised draft of my biographical findings, spending the days chasing up minor players in the drama. The results were almost invariably negative. The third Mrs Waldo Frank, who had 'gotten to know Waldo around 1940', told me that, as far as she knew, her husband's friendship with Evelyn had ended in the mid-thirties. There can have been little postwar contact and Mrs Frank knew nothing of Waldo's part in the fund which brought Evelyn and John back to America.

I also spoke to Philip Reisman, the once fanatical young communist who told Evelyn that, come the American revolution, she would be first to be shot. Though she had liked Mr Reisman in spite of this, the statement grew in importance as her paranoia worsened. In later years she would declare that 'the communists have told me that I will be first to be shot', as if this were an edict issued by some shadowy chain of command and not the hot-headed utterance of a single young man irritated by a fellow guest. Mr Reisman, who seemed a model of amiability, remembered being at Yaddo in 1933 and remembered a few fellow guests there, though not Evelyn Scott.

The hotel had changed ownership several times since 1963 and no record remained of which room the couple occupied. The owner of a nearby typewriter shop recalled that several writers had lived there in the fifties but, though he had been in business for thirty years, could not remember Evelyn Scott. The former manageress of the hotel, now retired, still lived on the premises, but she too remembered nothing of her. Evelyn Scott proved as absent from the place of her death as she had been from her birthplace.

One day in the communal kitchen I met an old lady who had been a resident since 1945. I told her of my researches and she told me her life story. She was the wife of a once affluent newspaper proprietor who had gone bankrupt many years ago.

'What can you do? You sell your real estate to pay off debts when prices are low and pretty soon you wind up with nothing. This woman. Did she mix much? What kind of woman was she anyway?'

I imagined her in the context of this shabby down-at-heel hotel and felt that her reborn aristocratic hauteur would have kept her from socialising.

'She would have been slightly odd in her manner I suppose, but not noticeably deranged. I don't think she would have been like the crowd in the lobby. She would have been too proud, too conscious of her fall in status. She was born in a big Southern mansion with a lot of servants. I think she would have kept herself to herself while here.'

The woman turned around from the stove to face me and made a stabbing gesture with her finger.

'Listen. There's a lot of people in this hotel who rode around in limousines once. A lot of us. And you know what? We all wound up here.'

The Definition Press had shown an interest in reprinting *A Calendar of Sin* in the mid-fifties and, learning that they still existed, I telephoned their SoHo address and asked if they were interested in reviving the idea.

They were equivocal about the possibility but told me that Mr Siegel, the founder, had always said if reprints were done, that book should be first. I asked what books they normally published.

'We publish books on the philosophy of aesthetic realism,' came the answer.

Well, that was the way they talked down in SoHo, I thought. I made an appointment to meet the directors the following day.

The Definition Press was part of a complex including a gallery, set in the modish depths of SoHo. I expected the gallery to contain examples of what passes for art in lower Manhattan and was mildly surprised to find realistic rural watercolours on show. I was directed upstairs to meet the directors; two ladies who wore badges proclaiming that they were 'victims of the press'.

Discussion did not get far before I felt that things were not as they seemed. The name of Mr Siegel was often reverentially invoked and the term 'aesthetic realism' seemed to crop up frequently. I looked at the badges again. Both ladies were past the age at which people habitually wear their hearts on their lapels.

'Could you explain the badges, please?'

The floodgates opened. It seemed that Aesthetic Realism was an all-embracing philosophy, created by Mr Siegel and propounded by him until his death in 1978. It was not better known because of a vast conspiracy to suppress his thought, hence the badges worn by his followers.

'Could you explain Mr Siegel's thought briefly?' I asked.

'Well, he believes that each of us consists of opposites which we're constantly trying to reconcile,' explained one lady. 'Does that sound strange to you?' she queried.

I had to confess that it sounded commonplace. I knew Eli Siegel as the author of a single poem, *Hot Afternoons Have Been in Montana*, a crossbreed of Walt Whitman and surrealism which won the 1925 *Nation* Poetry Prize. At some stage in his career Eli Siegel had made the leap, often fantasised but rarely realised, from poet to prophet. The Foundation for Aesthetic Realism was the result. Life is too short for many things; among these is room here for a detailed exposition of Mr Siegel's thought. However, to his followers he was (I quote their literature) 'the greatest human being who has ever lived' and only conspiracy has kept his ideas from a wider public. I was told that in the mid-fifties Evelyn attended some of Siegel's seminars, but had then stopped coming.

'Why?' I enquired.

'She went back to England,' said one of the women.

I assured her this was not so and the other woman confirmed this. 'She wasn't the woman she once was,' she suggested by way of explanation and I had to agree. Eli Siegel admired her work because of the way opposites were played against one another then reconciled as art. But, the woman observed, she had failed to reconcile the opposites in her own life. Once more I had to agree.

In fact I did not argue at all. I was silenced by the supreme irony that this institution, convinced that its failure to communicate was due to conspiratorial machinations, was the only one in the United States where the work of Evelyn Scott was actively studied. I learned more than I cared to know about Aesthetic Realism and the conspiracy to suppress it and, finally, I extricated myself. I gave Aesthetic Realists a spare copy of *Migrations* and they gave me a book of Siegel's verse and a pile of leaflets on their philosophy.

I stepped into the dusk settling over Greene Street feeling that, for whatever reason Evelyn had broken with these people, I was glad she had done so. The veracity or otherwise of Siegel's thought scarcely mattered. What was important was that, even in the final years of isolation, she would sit at no one's feet, not even those of the greatest man who has ever lived. I could feel some sympathy for the deluded followers who could only explain their failure to communicate by erecting a conspiracy against them. This was, after all, the miracle zone of art, where a painted plank with the right critical pedigree could retail for the price of a hardware store. Who, among this, could lay claim to possession of aesthetic truth?

No one knew where Evelyn Scott was buried. Creighton had severed communication with his mother by 1963 and funeral expenses were borne by Gladys Edgerton Grant, one of Lola Ridge's circle and a friend of Evelyn since the twenties. She too was dead and had left no record of the site of Evelyn's grave.

Learning this proved as simple as going to the nearest funeral director to the hotel and asking if they buried Evelyn Scott Metcalfe on August 6, 1963. They had done so, at Rose Hill Cemetery, Linden, New Jersey.

The following day I took a tortuous bus ride on my last journey of enquiry. I arrived in late afternoon, minutes before the cemetery offices closed. They told me she was buried in grave 45, section 68a, and indicated the site on a map. It was a quarter of a mile away on the other side of the graveyard.

Walking through the deserted plots on a chill November evening I tried, and failed, to generate a sense of occasion. The grave was unmarked; even its number tag had been torn off by a careless lawnmower. I had spent five years investigating the life of Evelyn Scott, yet photographing this featureless area of grass only deepened the absurdity. I had uncovered the last unknown fact, but the key to her personality still eluded me.

'I suppose you must know her fairly well by now?' a friend asked before I left for New York. I confessed I didn't and consoled myself with the thought that no one ever had. Each veil I removed revealed another veil and she remained the mass of contradictions who had puzzled Kay Boyle in Paris, sixty years ago.

'Bring her to life', I was advised by an editor who saw early drafts of my biographical notes. Who was I to bring to life? The libertarian friend of Emma Goldman or the FBI informant? The 'desperately intellectual' person Kay Boyle met, or the warm, generous person Geoffrey Grigson knew? The rebel who tried to put into practice standards of absolute personal freedom, or the martinet who beat her son with a hairbrush and nagged him for hiccoughing? The apostle of free love who pretended her lovers were her husbands? Anarchist or Republican? Political visionary or reactionary? Monster or near-saint? The Siegelians were right; it was not my task to make a posthumous unity of qualities she had failed to hold together in life. I could not reconcile her contradictions any more than I could reconcile the changing styles of the novels, the different voices used in letters to different people and the changes in physical appearance evidenced in the photographs. I could only present the facts as I had uncovered them.

The only key to the past is the present; that is, the lived experience of the perceiver. I had grown up in a time of upheaval believing that it represented an absolute break with past history. These feelings died with the passage of time, yet only when I examined twenties Bohemian life did I understand that it had all happened before, as I was often told, but never believed. The messianism, the experimentation in all fields, the sense of a complete rejection of the past and, inevitably, the casualties: all these had emerged in the twenties and died back also. I had investigated the life of a casualty; of two casualties if Creighton were included. The infant 'Jigeroo' seemed reminiscent in many ways of the dungareed children one met in communes, bemused by a shifting pack of adult faces and often burdened for life by a fanciful name. The judgement of these children on their parents is yet to be written.

I had uncovered a story of failure, and American literature is hard on its failures. In illuminating aspects of the concealed underbelly of American cultural life in this century, I hoped to expose the lie that literary history consists of a number of critically erected giants towering above a deserted landscape. The failures were a surer link to the past than those who self-consciously occupy central roles in their lifetimes, assured of posterity.

Bibliography

Evelyn Scott

Autobiography

Escapade. New York: Seltzer, 1923; New York: Cape & Smith, 1929/London: Cape, 1930.

Background in Tennessee. New York: McBride, 1937; Knoxville: University of Tennessee Press, 1980 (with an introduction by Robert L. Welker).

Novels

The Narrow House. New York: Boni & Liveright, 1921/London: Duckworth, 1921; New York: Arno Press, 1978 (with an introduction by Elizabeth Hardwick).

Narcissus. New York: Harcourt, Brace, 1922; New York: Arno Press, 1978 (with an introduction by Elizabeth Hardwick).

Bewilderment (British title for *Narcissus*). London: Duckworth, 1922.

The Golden Door. New York: Seltzer, 1925.

Ideals. New York: Boni, 1927.

Migrations. New York: Boni, 1927/London: Duckworth, 1927.

The Wave. New York: Cape & Smith, 1929/London: Cape, 1929.

A Calendar of Sin. New York: Cape & Smith, 1931.

Eva Gay. New York: Smith & Haas, 1933/London: Lovat Dickson, 1933.

Breathe Upon These Slain. New York: Smith & Haas, 1934/London: Lovat Dickson, 1934.

Bread and a Sword. New York: Scribner, 1937.

The Shadow of the Hawk. New York: Scribner, 1941.

Poetry

Precipitations. New York: Brown, 1920.

The Winter Alone. New York: Cape & Smith, 1930.

For children

In the Endless Sands (with Cyril Kay-Scott). New York: Holt, 1925.

Witch Perkins. New York: Holt, 1929.

Blue Rum (written under the pseudonym 'Ernest Souza'). New York: Cape & Smith, 1930.

Billy the Maverick. New York: Holt, 1934.

Creighton Scott

The Muscovites. New York: Scribner, 1940.

Confessions of an American Boy. Unpublished typescript in the possession of Paula Scott.

Cyril Kay Scott/Kay-Scott

Blind Mice. New York: Doran, 1921.

Sinbad. A Romance. New York: Seltzer, 1923.

Siren. London: Faber & Gwyer, 1925.

In the Endless Sands (with Evelyn Scott). New York: Holt, 1925.

Life is too Short. Philadelphia: Lippincott, 1943.

John Metcalfe

The Smoking Leg. London: Jarrolds, 1925.

Spring Darkness. London: Constable, 1928.

Arm's Length. London: Constable, 1930.

Judas and other Stories. London: Constable, 1931.

Brenner's Boy. London: White Owl Press, 1932.

Foster Girl. London: Constable, 1936.

All Friends Are Strangers. London: Nicholson & Watson, 1948.

The Feasting Dead. Sauk City, Wisconsin: Arkham House, 1954.

My Cousin Geoffrey. London: Macdonald, 1956.

Unpublished manuscripts of work in the library of the Humanities Research Center, Austin, Texas, include three novels, *Before Cock Crow, Escape into Living* and *The Grey Riddle,* and two books of verse, *The Gravestones Wept* and *The Youngest Smiles.* There are drafts of three playlets, unpublished and apparently unperformed, *An American Fantasy, Shadow Play* and *Second Shadow Play.* The unpublished manuscript of *Love* (alternatively titled *Conscience*), a play in three acts produced by the Provincetown Players in the Seventh Season, February 28 to March 13, 1921, is also held there.

The Humanities Research Center is the single most important source of Evelyn Scott manuscript material though researchers will also find much of interest in the Lola Ridge papers held in the Sophia Smith Collection at Smith College, Northampton, Mass. Thanks to Emma Goldman's considerate habit of retaining carbon copies of her correspondence, both sides of the Scott/ Goldman letters may be found at the International Institute for Social History in Amsterdam. The Scott/Gannett correspondence is housed among the Gannett papers at the Houghton Library, Harvard, Mass.

Other manuscript material of lesser importance may be located at the Beinecke Rare Book and Manuscript Library, Yale University, the Library of the University of Delaware, the Robert L. Woodruff Library at Emory University, the Newberry Library of the University of Chicago, the Delyte W. Morris Library at Southern Illinois University, the Rare Book Room of the University of Illinois at Urbana, Amherst College Library, the Library of the University of Michigan at Ann Arbor, the Poetry Collection of the State University of New York at Buffalo, the John M. Olin Library of Cornell University, the Lucy Scribner Library at Skidmore College, the George Arents Research Library at Syracuse University, the Western Reserve Historical Society Library of Cleveland, Ohio, the Charles Patterson Van Pelt Library at the University of Pennsylvania, the Alderman Library of the University of Virginia and the Lilly Library at Indiana University.

My thanks are due to the librarians of all these institutions for their co-operation and, where applicable, for permission to reproduce copyright material held by them.

A complete bibliography of the many poems, stories and critical articles published in magazines by Evelyn Scott would be lengthy and very largely an exercise in redundancy. Most of this material could be consulted only by those with access to the larger American University libraries or the Library of Congress. Those interested are advised to consult the bibliography of Robert L. Welker's unpublished 1958 doctoral thesis on Evelyn Scott, 'Evelyn Scott: A Literary Biography', submitted to the graduate school of Vanderbilt University. This is available from University Microfilms International, Ann Arbor, Michigan.

Index

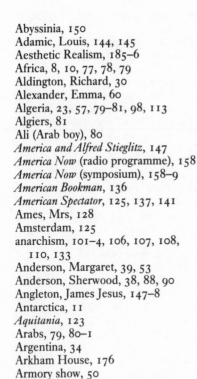

Index